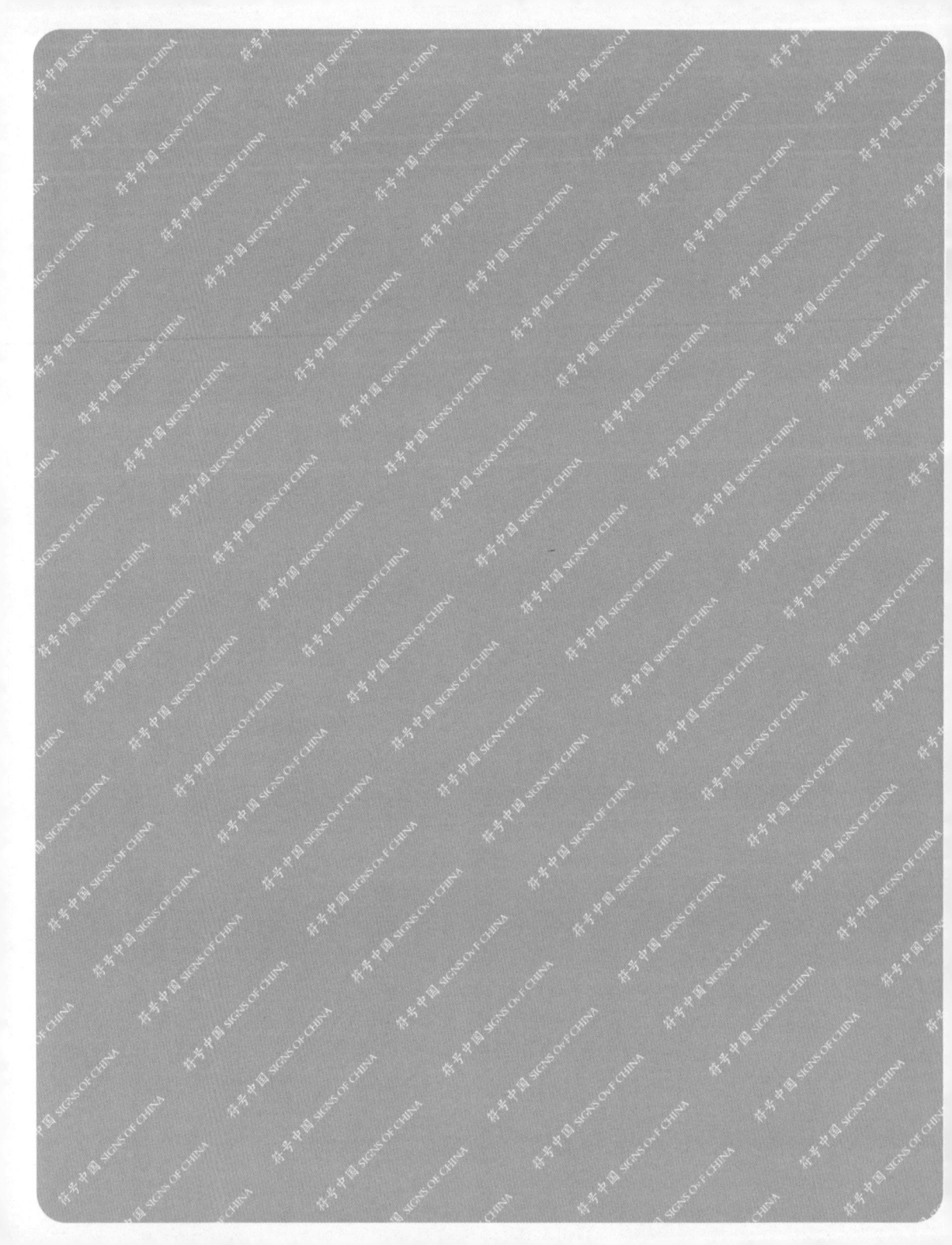

符号中国 SIGNS OF CHINA

# 大运河

## THE GRAND CANAL

"符号中国"编写组 ◎ 编著

中央民族大学出版社
China Minzu University Press

图书在版编目(CIP)数据

大运河：汉文、英文 /"符号中国"编写组编著. —北京：
中央民族大学出版社, 2024.3
（符号中国）
ISBN 978-7-5660-2292-9

Ⅰ.①大… Ⅱ.①符… Ⅲ.①大运河—介绍—中国—汉、英 Ⅳ.①K928.42

中国国家版本馆CIP数据核字（2024）第016885号

## 符号中国：大运河 THE GRAND CANAL

| 编　　著 | "符号中国"编写组 |
|---|---|
| 策划编辑 | 沙　平 |
| 责任编辑 | 李苏幸 |
| 英文指导 | 李瑞清 |
| 英文编辑 | 邱　械 |
| 美术编辑 | 曹　娜　郑亚超　洪　涛 |
| 出版发行 | 中央民族大学出版社 |
| | 北京市海淀区中关村南大街27号　邮编：100081 |
| | 电话：（010）68472815（发行部）　传真：（010）68933757（发行部） |
| | 　　　（010）68932218（总编室）　　　　（010）68932447（办公室） |
| 经销者 | 全国各地新华书店 |
| 印刷厂 | 北京兴星伟业印刷有限公司 |
| 开　本 | 787 mm×1092 mm　1/16　印张：10.25 |
| 字　数 | 131千字 |
| 版　次 | 2024年3月第1版　2024年3月第1次印刷 |
| 书　号 | ISBN 978-7-5660-2292-9 |
| 定　价 | 58.00元 |

版权所有　侵权必究

**"符号中国"丛书编委会**

唐兰东　巴哈提　杨国华　孟靖朝　赵秀琴

**本册编写者**

吴顺鸣

# 前言 Preface

京杭大运河是世界上最长的一条人工河道，它的开凿最早可以追溯到公元前5世纪春秋战国时代吴国的邗沟，到了一千多年前的隋代首次实现了南北贯通。京杭大运河北起北京，南达杭州，流经北京、河北、天津、山东、江苏、浙江6个省市，沟通了海河、黄河、淮河、长江、钱塘江五大水系，在中华民族的历史上，为南北方的交流与沟通做出了巨大的贡献。

The Grand Canal is the longest man-made canal of the world. The first establishment of the canal can be traced back to the Hangou Canal excavated by the State of Wu in the 5th century B.C. during the Spring and Autumn and Warring States periods. By the Sui Dynasty over 1000 years ago, the canal had connected the northern and southern China, and stretched from Beijing in the north to Hangzhou in the south. Flowing through 6 provinces and municipalities including Beijing, Hebei, Tianjin, Shandong, Jiangsu and Zhejiang, and uniting the 5 major water systems of the Haihe River, Yellow River, Huaihe River, Yangtze River and Qiantang River, the Grand Canal made enormous contribution to the communication between the north and south in Chinese history. This man-made river had not only provided transportation convenience for

正是这条人工长河，不仅为中华民族提供了舟楫之利，而且在其流经之地，人们靠运河之水灌溉排涝，使万顷碱滩成为沃野。运河还造就了两岸无数的城镇，使这些地区成为商贾云集、物阜民丰的繁盛之地。

本书通过追溯大运河开凿的历史，讲述大运河在千年间的繁荣与发展，介绍运河沿岸的名城，以及当地的民风民俗，旨在向读者展现一条包容、开放、魅力无穷的大运河。

the Chinese nation, but also fertilized the extensive saline-alkali soil into fertile lands. Further more, the canal brought up countless cities, making them the lands of prosperity.

By reviewing the excavation history of the Grand Canal, this book represents the prosperity and development of the Grand Canal in thousand of years, introduces the major cities and folk customs in the canal basin, aiming to unfold a comprehensive, patulous and charming Grand Canal to the readers.

# 目录 Contents

## 中国早期的运河
## Primitive Canals of China ............ 001

### 最早的运河
### Earliest Canal ............ 002

### 春秋战国时期的运河
### Canals of the Spring and Autumn and Warring States Periods ............ 005

### 秦汉时期的运河
### Canals of the Qin and Han Dynasties ............ 016

### 魏晋南北朝的运河
### Canals of the Wei, Jin and Southern and Northern Dynasties ............ 024

## 大运河的贯通与兴衰
## Cutthrough and Vicissitude of the Grand Canal ...... 029

### 隋代大运河的贯通
### Cutthrough of the Grand Canal in the Sui Dynasty ............ 030

### 唐宋大运河的繁荣
### Prosperity of the Grand Canal in the Tang and Song Dynasties ............ 041

元代大运河的定型
Finalization of the Grand Canal in the
Yuan Dynasty .................................................. 053

明代大运河的维护
Maintenance of the Grand Canal in the
Ming Dynasty .................................................. 061

清代大运河的衰落
Decline of the Grand Canal in the Qing Dynasty ....... 068

大运河的新生
Rebirth of the Grand Canal ................................ 075

## 大运河与中国名城
The Grand Canal and Its Major Cities ................. 077

北京
Beijing ............................................................ 078

天津
Tianjin ............................................................ 084

沧州
Cangzhou ....................................................... 092

德州
Dezhou ........................................................... 095

临清
Linqing ........................................................... 099

济宁
Jining ............................................................. 103

聊城
Liaocheng ...................................................... 108

淮安
Huai'an ............................................................ 112

扬州
Yangzhou ........................................................ 116

镇江
Zhenjiang ........................................................ 121

无锡
Wuxi ................................................................ 124

苏州
Suzhou ............................................................ 128

嘉兴
Jiaxing ............................................................. 136

杭州
Hangzhou ........................................................ 141

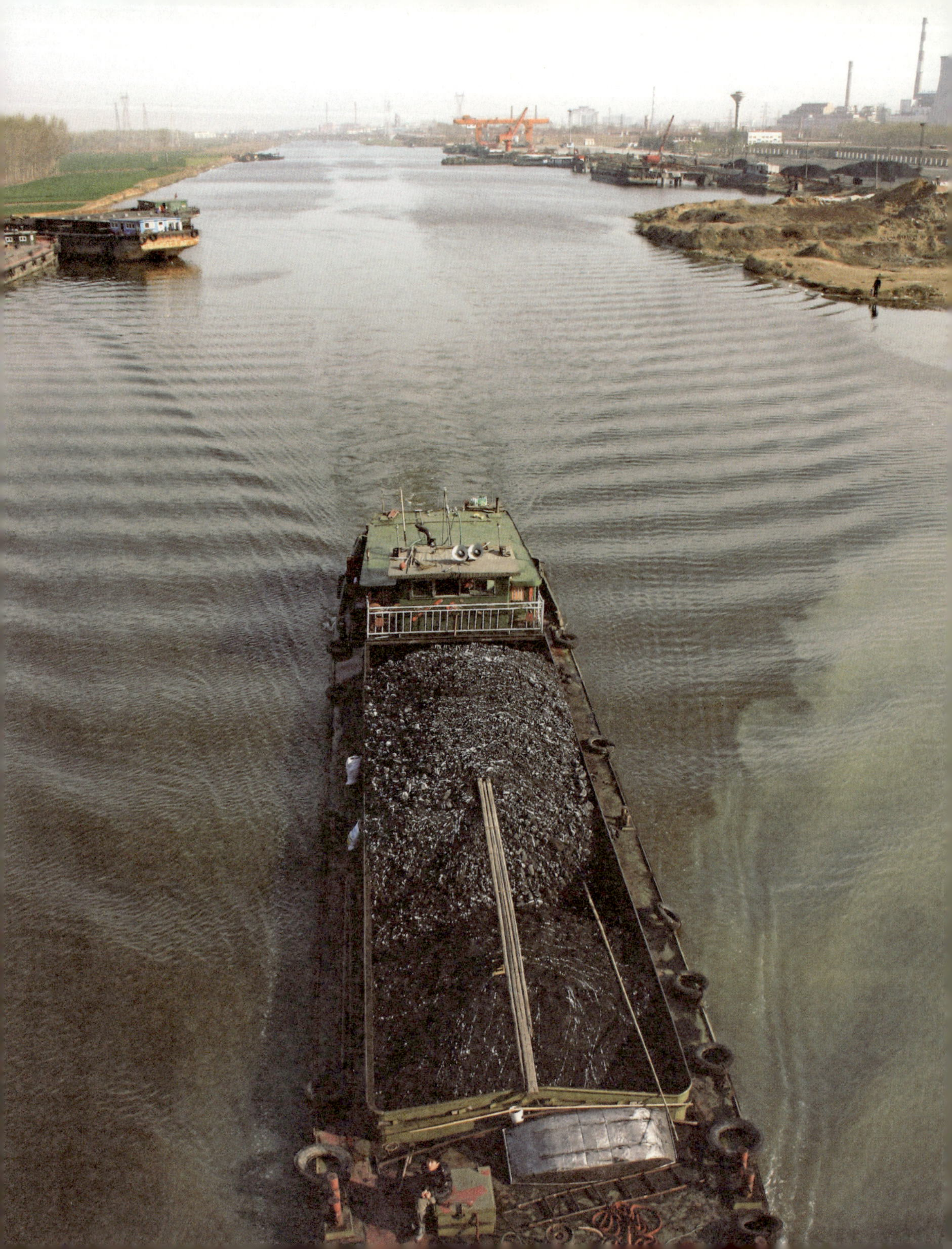

# 中国早期的运河
## Primitive Canals of China

在中国古代，人们很早就开始人工开凿运河。在远古传说中就有关于运河的最早记载。从春秋战国开始，中国人在这项改造自然的伟大工程中留下不少光辉的业绩。

In ancient times of China, people started to excavate man-made canals, which were first mentioned in the legends. By Spring and Autumn and Warring States periods, the Chinese nation had already made outstanding achievement in the great project of nature transforming.

## > 最早的运河

相传在4000多年前，中原地区洪水泛滥。当时的君王舜帝命禹治理洪水。禹带领人们开凿了"乃""冢"两条渠作为疏导洪水的渠道，将西北部奔涌而下的大洪水引向北方，减缓了洪水的流速，降低了洪水对下游的冲击力。之后禹又疏浚了九条大河，最终将洪水

- 青铜耒（商）
  耒是古代用来翻土的工具。
  Bronze *Lei* (Shang Dynasty, 1600B.C-1046B.C)
  *Lei* was an instrument used for cultivating in ancient times.

## > Earliest Canal

According to the legend, the flood was epidemic on the Central Plain over 4000 years ago. Shun, the king of that time, dispatched Yu to control the flood. Yu excavated the Naiqu Canal and Zhongqu Canal for the channelizing of the flood. The two canals directed the great flood rushing down the northwest region to the north, slowed down the flow rate, and reduced the impact force of the flood against the lower reaches. After then Yu successfully tamed the flood by dredging nine major rivers and eventually led the flood into the sea. Some people take the two canals as the beginning of China's canal history.

In the late Shang Dynasty in the 12th century B.C., the Zhou tribal leader King Tai of Zhou had three sons, the eldest son Taibo, the second son Zhongyong and the youngest son Jili. Understanding that the

浙江绍兴大禹陵
Yu Mausoleum in Shaoxing, Zhejiang Province

引入大海，成功地驯服了洪水。有人认为，这是中国人开凿运河的开始。

公元前12世纪的商朝末年，周部落的首领周太王有三个儿子，分别是长子泰伯、次子仲雍和三子季历。泰伯和仲雍兄弟二人看到父亲偏爱季历，为了将王位让给季历，于是便相继远赴南方蛮荒之地。泰伯就在今天江苏无锡的梅里地区

third son Jili was most favored by their father and in order to abdicate the throne to Jili, the brothers Taibo and Zhongyong successively left for the wild unsettled lands in the south. Taibo established the ancient kingdom of Gouwu, which subsequently developed to the State of Gouwu, in today's Meili region in Wuxi, Jiangsu Province. For the controlling of the flood, Taibo led the local ancestors to excavate the channel with nine tributaries

建立了勾吴古国，也就是后来的吴国。为了治理水患，泰伯带领当地先民在梅里一带开凿了西通太湖、东入漕湖的渠道，并挖掘了九条支流，既可抗旱涝灾害，又便利航运。这就是江南历史上第一条人工运河，人称"泰伯渎"，就是今天的伯渎港。

connecting the Taihu Lake in the west and Caohu Lake in the east. The channel was not only resistant to flood and drought disasters, but also convenient for shipping. People named the "Taibo Canal", which is today's Bodu Port. It's the first man-made canal in the history of the River South Region.

- **无锡古运河上的清名桥**（图片提供：微图）

清名桥原叫"清宁桥"，位于江苏无锡南门外的古运河与伯渎港交汇处，桥南侧是伯渎河，流经梅村至常熟。

**Qingming Bridge Crossing over the Ancient Canal in Wuxi**

The Qingming Bridge locates in the junction area of the ancient canal and the Bodu Port outside the South Gate of Wuxi in Jiangsu Province, and was used to be called the "Qingning Bridge". The Bodu Canal on the south of the bridge flows through Mei County to Changshu.

## > 春秋战国时期的运河

春秋时期，运河的开凿逐渐增多，有的为陈、蔡两国所开，在今淮水上游；有的为楚国所开，在今湖北、安徽境内；还有吴国所开的运河，位于太湖流域和长江、淮河、黄河之间。尤其是吴国开凿的几条运河，无论对当时及后代都有深远的影响。

春秋末年，在阖闾、夫差父子两代吴王的统治下，太湖流域有了初步开发，再加上有伍子胥、孙武等武将贤臣的襄助，国力渐强。为了取得霸权，吴王阖闾首先对越国、楚国两个邻国发动了战争。为了便于运兵运粮，公元前6世纪末至公元前5世纪初，吴国在天然河道的基础上，在太湖流域陆续凿成三条运河：一条叫胥浦，北起太

## > Canals of the Spring and Autumn and Warring States Periods

In the Spring and Autumn Period, the canal numbers increased. Some of the canals were dug by the states of Chen and Cai in today's upper reaches areas of the Huaihe River; some were dug by the State of Chu within the territory of today's Hubei and Anhui provinces; and some were excavated by the State of Wu in the Taihu Lake Basin surrounded by the Yangtze River, Huaihe River and Yellow River. Especially the several canals created by the State of Wu had exerted a far-reaching influence on that time and the future generations.

In the late Spring and Autumn Period, under the rule of the King of Wu, Helv and his son Fuchai, the Taihu Lake basin where the State of Wu located was firstly developed. Meanwhile with the

• 青铜吴王夫差盉（春秋）

这件铜盉高27.8厘米，腹径24.9厘米，肩上有一周铭文，大意是说吴王夫差用诸侯献给他的青铜，为一位女子铸了这件盉。盉的提梁设计成中空的龙形，龙身由无数纠缠的小龙组成，花纹如发丝般纤细，堪称鬼斧神工。

**Bronze *He* of Fuchai, the King of the Wu State** (Spring and Autumn Period, 770B.C.-221B.C)

This bronze *He* is 27.8 centimeters tall and the diameter of the belly is 24.9 centimeters. A circle of inscription on the vessel shoulder mentions that this *He* was made in bronze offered by the vassals and was a gift from the King Fuchai of Wu to a lady. The handle design of the wine vessel is a hollow dragon composing of innumerable tangled small dragons with slender patterns fine as hair, presenting the uncanny workmanship.

湖东面，南到杭州湾；一条叫胥溪，位于太湖西面，沟通了太湖和长江；还有一条由吴北上，到今江阴西部与长江会合。这些运河的开凿，不仅促进了区域性的

supporting of some loyal ministers like Wu Zixu and Sun Wu, etc, the national power of the State of Wu was enhanced. In order to chase the supremacy, the King Helv of Wu firstly started the war against the states of Yue and Chu. From the end of the 6th century B.C. to the beginning of the 5th century B.C., for the convenience of replenishment, the State of Wu continuously excavated three canals on the basis of the natural rivers in the Taihu Lake Basin, which were the Xupu Canal, starting from the eastern Taihu Lake in the north to the Hangzhou Bay in the south; the Xuxi Canal, locating to the west of Taihu Lake and connecting the Taihu Lake and the Yangtze River; and the third canal flowing north and entering into the Yangtze River in today's western Jiangyin. The excavation of these canals not only promoted the regional unity, but also laid the preliminary foundation of the subsequent River South canals.

In 506 B.C. and 494 B.C., the army of Wu successively defeated the states of Chu and Yue. The King Fuchai of Wu considered himself of already the master of the Yangtze River basin and decided to assault the north in order to further dominate the Central Plains. In

统一，而且为后来的江南运河奠定了初步基础。

公元前506年和前494年，吴军先后大败楚、越两国，吴王夫差认为自己在长江流域的霸主地位已经确立，决定向北方用兵，以进一步称霸中原。公元前486年，吴王下令建筑邗城，就是今天江苏扬州的前身，城址在今扬州市西北郊一带。接下来，吴国又从邗城西南引长江水，开凿了通往淮河的运河——邗

486 B.C., the King of Wu gave orders to build Hancheng, the predecessor of today's Yangzhou in Jiangsu Province, in today's northwest suburbs of Yangzhou. After that, the State of Wu brought in the water of the Yangtze River from the southwest of Hancheng and excavated the Hangou Canal connecting the Huaihe River. The canal is 150 kilometers long and is the first large man-made canal of China and the world with precise record of excavation time. With the history of

• 江苏扬州的古邗沟遗址（图片提供：FOTOE）
Ancient Hangou Relic in Yangzhou, Jiangsu Province

● 太湖风光
Scenery of Taihu Lake

沟。这是中国乃至世界上有确切开凿时间的第一条大型人工运河,长约150多千米。邗沟首次将中国东部的两条水系长江和淮河贯通起来,是后世大运河的重要基础,距今已有2400多年的历史。后世的两汉、隋、唐等朝代全用这条水道展开漕运,将江南的粮食输往京师。

邗沟凿通后,吴王夫差率领吴

over 2400 years, the Hangou Canal firstly linked the Yangtze River and Huaihe River, the two major water systems in eastern China, and laid a solid foundation for the excavation of the Grand Canal. In the later ages of the Han, Sui and Tang dynasties, this canal was used for grain transportation from the River South Region to the capitals.

After the finishing of the Hangou

## 卧薪尝胆

　　春秋后期，长江下游的吴国和越国相继强盛起来。两国为了扩张势力、逐鹿中原，进行了多年的争霸战争。公元前494年，吴王夫差进攻越国，将越王勾践围困于会稽（今浙江绍兴），迫使越国屈服。勾践投降后，被带到吴国侍奉吴王，三年后才被放回越国。回国后，勾践立志报仇雪耻。为了防止眼前的安逸生活消磨了志气，他在每顿饭前先尝一尝苦胆，还把睡觉垫的席子撤去，躺在柴草上面来锻炼自己的意志，这就是后来被人传诵的"卧薪尝胆"的故事。为了复兴越国，勾践重用贤臣范蠡和文种，并亲自参加耕种，救济贫苦的百姓。越国上下一心，经过十几年的努力，国力逐渐转弱为强。公元前473年，勾践调集精兵进攻吴国，大获全胜，最终灭掉了吴国。直至今日，中国人还经常用"卧薪尝胆"这个成语来形容人为了实现目标而刻苦自励、发愤图强的精神。

● 卧薪尝胆
Sleeping on Firewood and Tasting Gall

## Sleeping on Firewood and Tasting Gall

In the late Spring and Autumn Period, the states of Wu and Yue in the lower reaches regions of the Yangtze River successively became stronger. In order to expand the territories and fight for the throne, the two countries conducted wars against each other for years. In 494 B.C., the King Fuchai of Wu assaulted the State of Yue, by surrounding the King Goujian of Yue at Kuaiji (today's Shaoxing in Zhejiang Province), compelled the State of Yue to surrender. After then, Goujian was brought to the State of Wu to serve the King of Wu for three years. When returning home, Goujian swore to revenge. In order to prevent the spirit perishing from the life of ease, he tasted galls before meals, and took away the mat and sleep on the firewood to train his willpower, which is widely read as "Sleeping on Firewood and Tasting Gall". For the reviving of the State of Yue, Goujian took the advice of some loyal ministers like Fan Li and Wen Zhong, attended farming in person, and relieved the poor people. With the national unity and more than ten years' striving, the national power changed from weak to strong. In 473 B.C., Goujian commanded picked troops assaulting the State of Wu, gained a complete victory and destroyed the State of Wu. Until today, the Chinese people still use the phrase of "Sleeping on Firewood and Tasting Gall" to describe the striving spirit.

国的那些经过"兵圣"孙武亲自调教过的军队，顺流北上，经淮河，入泗水，大举伐齐。齐国在吴军的强大攻势下，节节败退，吴王夫差由此威震中原。如果不是越王勾践趁吴国空虚入侵吴国，迫使吴王夫差紧急回国平乱，他完全可能一举歼灭齐国，成为新的中原霸主。

战国时期的魏国地处黄河和淮河两大水系之间的平原地带，土地肥沃，国富兵强。魏惠王继位后，

Canal, the King Fuchai of Wu led the army disciplined by Sun Wu, the Ultimate Master of War, heading northward downstream, passing through the Huaihe River and entering into the Sishui River, to massively assault the State of Qi. Facing with the strong offensive of the Wu army, the State of Qi retreated one step after another, thus the name of Fuchai was well known all over the Central Plains. If not for the invasion by the King Goujian of Yue into the State of Wu compelling Fuchai imminently

**河南荥阳的古鸿沟遗址** （图片提供：FOTOE）
Ancient Honggou Canal Relic in Xingyang, Henan Province

returning home for the quelling of the rebellion, he probably had already destroyed the State of Qi and became the new master of the Central Plains.

The State of Wei in the Warring States Period located in the plain region between the two water systems of the Yellow River and the Huaihe River with fertile soil, powerful national strength and strong army. After inheriting the throne, the King Hui of Wei gave order to excavate canal from Xingyang County in Henan Province, introducing the water of the Yellow River. The canal flew to the east through Zhengzhou and Kaifeng, then turned south and flew through Huaiyang, at last entered into the Yingshui River, one of the tributaries of the Huaihe River. After completing the project, the King Hui of Wei named it the "Honggou Canal". The Honggou Canal connecting the Yellow River in the north and the Huaihe River in the south was

下令从河南省荥阳县开凿运河，将黄河水引出，向东经过郑州、开封，又转向南，经过淮阳到达颍水，与淮河相连。工程竣工之后，魏惠王将这条运河命名为"鸿沟"。鸿沟施工时，魏国不仅在自己国内开凿，而且将工程开到了其他国家境内。魏国周边的宋、郑、

## 楚河汉界

秦朝灭亡之后，从公元前206年到公元前202年，以西楚霸王项羽和汉王刘邦为首的两大军事集团为争夺天下，进行了一系列大规模战争，史称"楚汉之争"。前205年，刘邦进驻荥阳城（今河南荥阳），从此，汉军和楚军在荥阳一带展开了拉锯战，双方爆发大小战役数十次，各有胜负。公元前203年，楚军与汉军讲和，双方约定以黄河南岸的运河鸿沟为界，"中分天下"，以西为汉，以东为楚。在中国象棋棋盘上对战双方之间有一个空白的区域，写有"楚河""汉界"字样，就是由此得来的。

## Border of Chu and Han

After the Qin Dynasty perished, from 206 B.C. to 202 B.C., the two political and military groups respectively leading by the "King of Western Chu" Xiang Yu and the "Lord of Han" Liu Bang conducted a epic warfare to fight the world, which is recorded as the "Chu-Han Contention" in the history. In 205 B.C., Liu Bang entered and garrisoned in Xingyang Castle (today's Xingyang in Henan Province). Since then, the armies of Han and Chu conducted years of seesaw battle in the Xingyang region. After dozens of campaigns in different sizes, the two parties were neck and neck. In 203B.C., the Chu army reluctantly negotiated peace with the Han army. The both parties promised to "split the world" by the Honggou Canal to the south bank of the Yellow River. The western of the canal belonged to Han and the eastern of the canal belonged to Chu. There is a blank zone on the Chinese Chess chessboard between the domains of the two sides marked with the words of "Chu River" and "Han Border", which come from the Chu-Han Contention.

• 中国象棋
Chinese Chess

蔡、曹、卫等国境内都修造了一段南下淮河和北上黄河的河道。这条运河的建成，使黄淮平原上形成了一条便利的水上交通线，沿岸各国的农业、手工业都得到了较大的发展。

战国后期，秦国在诸侯争霸中渐渐脱颖而出，秦国的东邻韩国随时都有被秦并吞的可能。公元前

not only constructed within the territory of Wei, but also extended into the states of Song, Zheng, Cai, Cao and Wei. The built of this canal formed a convenient water traffic line on the Huanghuai Plain and extremely boosted the agriculture and handicraft industries of the countries by the riverside.

In the late Warring States Period, as the State of Qin had gradually stood out

- 陕西泾阳的泾河（图片提供：微图）
郑国渠首遗址位于泾阳县城西25千米处的泾河东岸。
Jinghe River in Jingyang, Shaanxi Province
The head of Zhengguo Canal relic locates in the eastern bank of the Jinghe River 25 kilometers west to Jingyang County.

• 十二字砖（秦）

这块铭文砖长30.8厘米、宽26.7厘米，正面以凸线划分为12个方格，每格内有一秦篆，为"海内皆臣，岁登成熟，道毋饥人"，是歌功颂德之词。

**Twelve Characters Brick (Qin Dynasty, 221B.C-206B.C)**

This inscriptive brick is 30.8 centimeters long and 26.7 centimeters wide. The surface of the brick is divided into twelve squares by ridges. In each square there is a character depicted in the ancient style of calligraphy adopted in the Qin Dynasty. The characters phrase the merits and achievements of the Qin Dynasty as "unification of the whole country, grain harvest, and none of starving people".

246年，韩王以著名的水利工程专家郑国为间谍，入秦游说秦王在泾水和渭水的支流北洛水间穿凿一条大型灌溉渠道。这是以发展秦国农业为诱惑的计谋，其真实目的是要消耗秦国的国力。郑国的游说很快打动了秦王，秦国调集了全国数十万民夫，并投入大量物力开凿运河，郑国被任命为运河工程的总负

from the princes vied for supremacy, the State of Han, the neighbouring country of Qin, was facing the threat of being absorbed by Qin. In 246 B.C., the king of Han dispatched a spy, the famous water conservancy project expert Zheng Guo, into the State of Qin to persuade the king of Qin into the excavation of a large irrigation canal connecting the tributaries of the Jingshui River and Weishui River. Developing agriculture was the bait, exhausting the national power of Qin was the real intention. Zheng Guo's idea touched the king of Qin in no time, and the king assembled a force of hundreds of thousands of people from all over the country and vast materials to excavate the canal. Zheng Guo was appointed as the project chief. During the construction, the conspiracy of the State of Han was uncovered. The king of Qin was furious and intended to send Zheng Guo to death. But Zheng Guo said, "Spy as I am, the canal construction will truly benefit the State of Qin. Although I prolonged the life of Han for several years, but have established immortal contribution to Qin." The king of Qin accepted his principle and kept putting Zheng Guo in the important position. After over 10 years' endeavor, the canal was completed

责人。在施工过程中，韩国的阴谋败露，秦王大怒，要杀郑国。郑国说："微臣虽然是间谍，但是修建渠道也确实对秦国有利，臣为韩国延长了数年之命，却为秦国建立了万世之功啊。"秦王认为郑国说得有道理，所以一如既往地对郑国加以重用。经过十多年的努力，全渠完工，人称"郑国渠"。郑国渠所流经的地域，四万多顷农田得到灌溉，粮食产量提高。运河不仅没有拖垮秦国，反而加速了秦国对外扩张的步伐。

郑国渠全长150千米，位于今天陕西泾阳县西北25千米处的泾河北岸，是秦代关中平原上的一条重要水上通道。它不仅灌溉了泾水流域的大面积农田，而且也促进了关中平原上的商业和手工业的发展。其后的秦、汉两代在关中建都与这条运河有着很大的关系，魏晋南北朝时期附近民众也都受益于这条运河。

and called the "Zhengguo Canal", which irrigated the over forty thousand *Qing* (a unit of area, 1 *Qing* equals to 6.6667 hectares) of farmlands in the basin areas of the canal and increased the grain production. The canal not only didn't drag down the national power of Qin, but also accelerated its expansion on the contrary.

The over 150 kilometers long Zhengguo Canal locates to the north bank of the Jinghe River 25 kilometers northwest to today's Jingyang County in Shannxi Province, and was a major water passageway on the Central Shaanxi Plain in the Qin Dynasty. The canal irrigated the vast farmlands in the Jingshui River basin, and enhanced the development of the commerce and handicraft industries of the Central Shaanxi Plain. It's also the reason for the later Qin and Han dynasties to choose their capitals in Central Shaanxi. Further more, the canal benefited people near by in the Wei, Jin and the Northern and Southern dynasties in the later ages.

## > 秦汉时期的运河

公元前221年，秦始皇统一中国，建立了历史上第一个统一的封建王朝——秦朝。公元前214年，秦军分五路南下，对居住在今两广地区的南越和西瓯进行大规模的战争。百越地带丛林密集，瘴气弥漫，又有五岭阻隔，大军前进得很艰难，军粮的供给更成问题。为了解决大军的粮食供应问题，秦始皇下令开凿一条连接湘水和漓水的运河，这就是著名的灵渠。这条运河是人类历史上有据可查的第一条穿越山脉的运河。

为了开凿这条运河，朝廷调集了50万民夫。河工们首先在兴安城（今广西兴安县）北的五龙山下修建起一道石堤，将湘江的上游河段海洋河分成两部，形成蓄水塘，之

## > Canals of the Qin and Han Dynasties

In 221 B.C., the First Emperor of Qin united China and established the Qin Dynasty, the first uniform feudal dynasty in the history. In 214 B.C., the Qin army assaulted south in five routes, started massive wars against the states of Southern Yue and Western Ou in today's Guangdong and Guangxi provinces. As forests, miasma and mountains spread all over the Yue region, it was difficult for marching and replenishment. In order to solve the supplying problem, the First Emperor of Qin gave order to excavate a canal linking the Xiangshui River and the Lishui River, which is the famous Lingqu Canal. This canal is the first one in human history that crosses the mountains and be well documented.

For the excavation of this canal, the court assembled half a million people. The

● 今日漓江山水
Today's Scenery of Lijiang River

后再分别凿成南、北两渠，北渠引水注入湘江，南渠将河水引出，经兴安城向西，与漓江相通。修建灵渠的工程非常复杂，尤其是南渠一路都是傍山而建，途中要破掉几座拦路的山崖，在跨越分水岭太史庙山时，更是要在几十米高的石山中劈开一条河道。这样的工程在当时的条件下完成实属不易。

灵渠建成后，秦始皇顺利挥师

workers firstly built up a stone dyke at the foot of the Wulong Mountain north to Xing'an Town (today's Xing'an County in Guangxi Province) which divided the Haiyang River, the upper reaches section of the Xiangjiang River, into two parts and formed the impounding reservoir, then respectively excavated the southern section and northern section. The northern section introduced the water into the Xiangjiang River, and the southern

- 百越文化双环首云纹青铜短剑（战国）
Bronze Short Sword with Double Ring Head Cloud Design of Yue Culture (Warring States Period, 475B.C-221B.C)

section directed the water out of Xing'an Town to the west and entering into the Lijiang River. The Lingqu Canal project was extremely complex, especially for the southern section. As the canal flew through the valleys, a few mountains had to be destroyed for the construction of the canal. At the watershed of Taishi Temple Mountain, a rocky mountain of dozens meters high was cleaved for a river way. Such project could not have been easy for the conditions of that time.

After the completion of the Lingqu Canal, the First Emperor of Qin assaulted

- 广西桂林兴安县的灵渠（图片提供：全景正片）
Lingqu Canal in Xing'an County, Guilin, Guangxi Zhuang Autonmous Region

百越，征服了中国南方。从那时起，从北方来的船舶便可以从长江经湘江进入灵渠的南渠，再由漓江、桂江进入珠江流域，直抵广州。在秦后的2000多年间，灵渠一直作为中国南方南北走向的一条水上主干线，对岭南地区的经济发展起着非常重要的作用。

公元前202年西汉建都长安（今西安市）后，朝廷的物资、粮食来源主要取自关中和关东。关东的漕粮需经黄河西入渭水，才能到达长安。但是渭河的河道不仅蜿蜒曲折，而且水位很浅，枯水季节无法通航，而且时有溃决或淤塞，长安的物资供应很难得到保障。为了解决这个问题，大司农郑当时便向汉武帝建议，从长安开凿一条新渠，

• 翻土用的铁锸（西汉）
Iron *Cha* Used for Cultivation (Western Han Dynasty, 206B.C-25A.D)

the Yue region and successfully conquered the Southern China. Since then, ships from the north could reach Guangzhou successively through the Yangtze River, Xiangjiang River, south Lingqu Canal, Lijiang River, Guijiang River and Zhujiang River basin. During the over two thousand years after the Qin Dynasty, the Lingqu Canal was consistently a north-south water trunk line in Southern China, and played an important role in the economic development of the Lingnan Region.

After the Western Han Dynasty made Chang'an (today's Xi'an City) the capital in 202 B.C., the supplies and grain from the court were mainly taken from the Central Shaanxi Plain and Northeast China. The grain from Northeast China should go through the Yellow River and Weihe River to reach Chang'an. But as the Weihe River channel was not only zigzag, but also shallow in water level, the ships could not pass in dry seasons. The materials supply of Chang'an was difficult to guarantee. In order to solve this problem, the minister of national treasury Zheng Dangshi advised the Emperor Wu of Han to excavate a new canal from Chang'an, directing the water of the Weihe River to the Yellow

## 雄才伟略的汉武帝

　　汉武帝刘彻（前156—前87）是一位具有雄才大略的帝王。在他统治时期，西汉王朝迎来了鼎盛繁荣的时期。汉武帝为削弱诸侯国的势力，颁布"推恩令"，允许诸侯王将封地再封给自己的子弟。在经济方面，他奖励农耕、发展生产，建立了煮盐、冶铁、运输和贸易的官营制度，并大力兴修水利，使西汉国力空前强大。汉武帝在位时，中国境内的汉、匈奴、西域各族、越族以及西南、东南、东北各族人民之间的经济文化交流进一步加强。汉武帝还曾两次派张骞出使西域，使汉朝与西域建立联系，初步打开了东西方交流的重要通路——丝绸之路，推动了东西方经济文化的交流。

## Emperor Wu of Han with Great Talent and Ambition

Liu Che (156 B.C.-87 B.C.), the Emperor Wu of Han, was an emperor with great talent and ambition. During his reign, the Western Han Dynasty reached its peak. For the impairing of

● 汉武帝茂陵（图片提供：全景正片）
Mausoleum of Emperor Wu of the Han Dynasty

the vassal states, the Emperor Wu of Han issued laws permitting the feudatory kings passing on the manors to their descendants. In the economic field, he encouraged farming, developed production, established the state-run system in salt, iron-smelting, transportation and trading fields, strived to develop the water conservancy, largely strengthened the national power of the Western Han Dynasty. During the reign of the Emperor Wu of Han, the economic and cultural communication among the Han and various ethnic groups within the territory of China was further enhanced. The Emperor Wu of Han also dispatched Zhang Qian to the Western Regions twice for diplomatic missions, built the relationships between the Han Dynasty and the Western Regions, and initially established the Silk Road, which was the important passageway linking the East and West and promoted the economic and cultural communication.

引渭河的水一直通至黄河。汉武帝采纳了他的建议，征调数万军民修渠。三年后漕渠建成，不仅缩短了漕粮运输距离（关东漕粮只需三个月就运达长安）、改善了航道，而且渠下民田万余顷皆得灌溉之利。

西汉时期，沟通全国的运河体系已初步形成，由漕渠、黄河、鸿沟、邗沟等构成的东西水运通道成为交通大动脉，每年由此运道输往关中的漕粮有400万至600万石。

公元25年，东汉王朝定都于河南洛阳。公元48年，光武帝下诏开凿阳渠。这条运河主要连接都城洛阳与黄河，各地漕船可直

River. The Emperor Wu of Han adopted his proposal and requisitioned tens of thousands of soldiers and civilians to excavate the canal. Three years later the Caoqu Canal was completed, which shorted the transport distance and improved the course. The grain from Northeast China could be shipped to Chang'an within only three months. Besides, the vast farmlands by the canal were also well irrigated.

In the Western Han Dynasty, the nationwide canal system was initially shaped. The east-west waterway transportation channel consisting of the Caoqu Canal, Yellow River, Honggou Canal, Hangou Canal and so on became

抵洛阳城下。阳渠的建成为洛阳的交通发展和工商业的繁荣创造了条件。

从西汉末年到东汉前期，黄河连年泛滥，原为鸿沟支流的汴渠向东溢流，淹没了数十郡县，两岸百姓怨声载道。公元69年，汉明帝命水利专家王景治理黄河、修治汴渠。王景亲自勘测地形，凿山引水，疏浚河床，还创造性地采用了许多有效疏导和防范洪水的办法。经过修治，汴渠在防洪、抗旱、灌

● 绿釉陶仓（东汉）
Green Glazed Pottery Bin (Eastern Han Dynasty, 25-220)

the transportation artery, conveying four million to six million *Dan* (a unit of dry measure for grain) of grain to the Central Shaanxi Plain per year.

In 25 A.D., the Eastern Han Dynasty made Luoyang in Henan Province the capital. In 48 A.D., the Emperor Guangwu issued an imperial edict to excavate the Yangqu Canal, which mainly connected the capital Luoyang and the Yellow River, assuring the ships from various regions to reach Luoyang shortly. The completion of the Yangqu Canal created conditions for the local transportation development and the prosperity of the local industry and commerce industries.

From the late Western Han Dynasty to the early Eastern Han Dynasty, the Yellow River was in flood for successive years. The Bianqu Canal, the tributary of the Honggou Canal, overflowed east and overwhelmed dozens of counties, which brought miserable life to the people living by the canal. In 69 A.D., the Emperor Ming of Han assigned the hydraulic expert Wang Jing to control the flood of the Yellow River and repair the Bianqu Canal. Wang Jing personally surveyed the topography, cut through mountains to direct the water, swept the riverbed, and adopted many creative and

● 流过古都洛阳的洛河（图片提供：全景正片）
Luohe River Flowing Through the Ancient Capital Luoyang

溉、航运和稳定黄河河道等方面都发挥了巨大作用。此后800多年间，黄河没有发生过大的水患。这些运河的开凿和治理，使洛阳成为当时全国的水运中心。

effective methods to dredge and prevent the flood. After the repairs, the Bianqu Canal played an important role in flood control, drought resisting, irrigation, shipping and stabilizing of the Yellow River channel. During the 800 years since then, there was no large flood coming up from the Yellow River. The excavation and maintenance of these canals made Luoyang the nationwide water transportation center at that time.

## > 魏晋南北朝的运河

魏晋南北朝时期，因国家长期处于南北分裂、军阀割据的状态，全国性运河体系的发展受到制约，但区域性的运河系统仍在不断拓展。

三国时期，曹魏政权在河北平原上开凿了白沟、利漕渠、平虏渠、泉州渠、新河等一系列运河，建立起以邺城（今河北磁县东南）为中心的河北平原水运网络，加强了长江、淮河、黄河、海河之间的水运联系。邺城漕船经由这些运河，向北可直抵河北平原北端的滦河下游，向南可由黄河抵达江淮，直至钱塘，至此，一条贯通南北的水运大通道初步形成。邺城很快就成为黄河以北最热闹繁华的大都市，各地人员和物资纷纷聚集到邺

## > Canals of the Wei, Jin and Southern and Northern Dynasties

During the Wei, Jin and Southern and Northern dynasties, as years' warfare, the country was separated between the north and the south, and the development of the nationwide canal system was restricted. But, on the other hand, the regional canal system was expanding.

In the Three Kingdoms Period, the Cao's regime excavated a series canals such as the Baigou Canal, Licao Canal, Pinglu Canal, Quanzhou Canal, Xinhe Canal and on the Hebei Plain, and also established the water transportation network there centered on Yecheng (southeast to today's Cixian County in Hebei Province), strengthening the water connection of the Yangtze River, Huaihe River, Yellow River and Haihe

**邺城金凤台遗址**（图片提供：FOTOE）

金凤台位于邺城西北隅，建于建安十八年（213年），原高八丈，为曹操大宴群臣、举行大典的主要场所。

**Golden Phoenix Platform Relics in Yecheng**

The Golden Phoenix Platform built in 213 A.D. locates in the northwest region in Yecheng, and was 8 *zhang* (a unit of length, 1 *Zhang* equal to 3.33 meters) high. The platform was used by the Emperor Wu of Wei to fete the ministers and hold the ceremonies.

城，城中人口最多时达到百万。此后的270多年里，后赵、前燕、北魏、东魏、北齐等政权相继在此建都。

公元245年，南方的东吴政权开凿了连接秦淮河和太湖的运河破冈渎。这条运河全长近千里，起点在当时东吴的都城建康（今南京市），凿穿句容山过云阳直奔东

River. With these canals, the ships from Yecheng could directly reach the Luanhe River downstream on the northern Hebei Plain in the north, and the Qiantang River in the Yangtze-Huaihe Region in the south through the Yellow River. Since then, a giant waterway transportation channel running south and north was initially shaped. Soon later, Yecheng

南，又经常州、无锡、苏州，一直到吴江、嘉兴等地，之后又经杭州连通钱塘江，最终到达春秋时越国的都城会稽（今浙江绍兴）。从这条运河南下，可以避免船只在长江的激流中航行的风险，而且航程也缩短了四分之一。西晋时期，当阳侯杜预开凿了扬口运河，加强了江汉地区的水运联系。东晋时的谢安、谢玄叔侄主持疏浚了苏北运河。而南朝齐则在东吴破冈渎的基

became the most prosperous metropolis in the north of the Yellow River. People and goods from various regions gathered in Yecheng, and the highest population was over one million. In the 270 years after that, various regimes including the Later Zhao, Former Yan, Northern Wei, Eastern Wei and Northern Qi all chose their capitals here in succession.

In 245 A.D., the Eastern Wu regime in south China excavated the Pogangdu Canal, which connected the Qinhuai River and the Taihu Lake and was nearly 500 kilometers long. The canal started from the capital city of the Eastern Wu, Jiankang (today's Nanjing), then cut through the Jurong Mountain and head southeast, passed through Yunyang, Changzhou, Wuxi, Suzhou, Wujiang, Jiaxing and Hangzhou to connect the Qiantang River, and at last arrived at Kuaiji (today's Shaoxing in Zhejiang Province), the capital of the Yue State in the Spring and Autumn Period. Heading down south on this canal, people could avoid the riptide of the Yangtze River and

• 东晋宰相谢安像
Portrait of Xie An, Prime Minister of the Eastern Jin Dynasty

### 浙江绍兴八字桥

八字桥位于绍兴城区，始建于南宋。桥坐落在三街、三河的交叉处，桥东为南、北落坡，成八字形；桥西为西、南落坡，成八字形；桥两端的南向两个落坡也成八字形，且坡下各有一个桥洞，又形成了两座小桥，被称为"古代的立交桥"。

### The Bazi Bridge in Shaoxing, Zhejiang Province

The Bazi Bridge locates in the downtown of Shaoxing and was firstly built in the Southern Song Dynasty. Seating at the junction area of three streets and three rivers, the bridge is in A-shape looking from three directions. Beneath the two southern slopes, there are two archways, forming another two tiny bridges. People praised it as the "ancient flyover".

础上进行延长，修建了丹徒水道，成为隋朝大运河江南运河段的前身。这一时期，运河沟通的范围更加广阔，一个以中原地区为中心，

shorten one quarter of the cruising range. In the Western Jin Dynasty, the marquis Du Yu excavated the Yangkou Canal, which improved the water transportation network in the Jianghan Region. In the Eastern Jin Dynasty, Xie An and his nephew Xie Xuan managed to dredge the Subei Canal. Qi Ze from the Southern dynasties built the Dantu Canal on the basis of the Pogangdu Canal excavated by the Eastern Wu regime, which was the predecessor of the Grand Canal River South section built in the Sui Dynasty. In this period, the communication range

● 夜色中的秦淮河
Night Scene of the Qinhuai River

北通涿郡（今北京）、南达岭南、西接关中的水运网络初步形成，为隋代大运河的开凿奠定了基础。

of the canal system was broadened. Centering on the Central Plains, the network could reach Zhuojun County (today's Beijing) to the north, Lingnan to the south and the central Shaanxi Plain to the west, laying the foundation for the Grand Canal.

## 大运河的贯通与兴衰
## Cutthrough and Vicissitude of the Grand Canal

　　三国两晋南北朝时期，北方人不断南迁，先进的生产技术随之南下。隋代，中国的经济重心逐渐从黄河流域转移到了长江中下游地区。为了满足中原地区和边防军队的粮食需求，开凿大运河将江淮地区的物资通过水路向北转运成为迫切需要。

During the Three Kingdoms Period, Eastern and Western Jin, and Northern and Southern dynasties, the northerners kept moving south, bringing the advanced production technologies with them. By the Sui Dynasty, the economic center had gradually moved from the Yellow River basin to the middle and lower reaches regions of the Yangtze River. In order to meet the food supply of the Central Plains and frontier armies, the Sui Dynasty was pressed to excavate the Grand Canal to transport the materials in the Yangtze-Huaihe Region to the north.

## ＞ 隋代大运河的贯通

公元581年，隋朝建立，定都大兴城（今陕西西安）。几年后，隋朝灭了南方的陈朝，结束了长达300多年的南北分裂局面，继秦朝后再一次统一了中国。隋朝立

• 隋文帝像
Portrait of Emperor Wen of Sui

## ＞ Cutthrough of the Grand Canal in the Sui Dynasty

The Sui Dynasty was established in 581 and chose Daxing City (today's Xi'an in Shaanxi Province) as capital. A few years later, Sui destroyed the Chen Dynasty in the south, terminated the 300 years' secession and reunified China once again since the Qin Dynasty. In the beginning of the foundation, to assure the supply of the capital, the Emperor Wen of Sui gave orders to excavate canal for the food transportation from the Yangtze-Huaihe Region to the capital.

The Caoqu Canal firstly built by the Emperor Wu of Han was reused. For the repeated wars during the over 700 years since the completion of the Caoqu Canal, the watercourse was silted up and difficult for shipping. The Emperor Wen of Sui intended to take use of this ready-made canal to carry out the water

黄釉陶女俑（隋）
Yellow Glazed Pottery Female Figurine
(Sui Dynasty, 581-618)

国之初，为了保证京师的供给，必须要将江淮地区的粮食物资运往京师，于是隋文帝下令修凿运河，展开漕运。

始建于汉武帝时期的漕渠在隋代被重新启用。漕渠自凿通之后700多年间，由于历经多次战乱，以致河道淤塞、难以行船。隋文帝要利用这条现成的运河，开水运直

transportation to the south. The project was managed by the minister Yuwen Kai. The rebuilt Caoqu Canal started from the capital to Tongguan County. The overall length was 200 kilometers. After the completion, this section of canal was renamed Guangtong Canal. The expenses of the transportation by this canal was hundreds of millions taels of silver cheaper per year than by road. Since then, the commercial intercourse between Chang'an and Tongguan became more and more prosperous, and the trade and industry were also well developed. No matter authority or common people all praised the excavation of this canal.

The general director of this canal Yuwen Kai not only dredged the riverbed of the Caoqu Canal built by the Han Dynasty, but also uniformly programmed the channel based on the foundation of the former riverbed. He set up a series of gate dams in the shipping lane to assure the water level of the canal, enabling giant ship with four masts and four sails to navigate. The excavation of this canal accumulated valuable technical experience of the Grand Canal built later.

At that time, Chen, the last regime of the Southern dynasties, had not been fully destroyed. Aiming to achieve to

通南方，工程由营新都副监宇文恺负责。重新开挖的漕渠从大兴城开始直至潼关，全长200千米。工程竣工后，这段漕渠被改名为"广通渠"。这条运河疏通后，比原来的陆路运输一年内可以节省上亿银两的运输费用。从此长安与潼关间的

complete reunification, the Emperor Wen of Sui intended to massively assault Chen. In 587, the Emperor Wen of Sui gave orders to excavate the Shanyangdu Canal, which started from Shanyang (today's Huai'an in Jiangsu Province) in the north to Hancheng (today's Yangzhou in Jiangsu Province) in the

- **陕西西安大兴善寺**
  位于西安市城南，始建于晋，初称遵善寺。隋文帝扩建长安城为大兴城时，遵善寺也得以扩建，并由隋文帝赐名大兴善寺。

  **Daxingshan Temple in Xi'an, Shaanxi Province**
  The temple locating in the southern area of Xi'an was firstly built in the Jin Dynasty and was named Zunshan Temple at first. When the Emperor Wen of Sui extended Chang'an into Daxing City, he expanded the Zunshan Temple once again and granted it the name of Daxingshan Temple.

商业往来更加频繁，工商业得到了极大的发展。无论官府还是百姓们，都对这条运河赞不绝口。

这条运河的总指挥宇文恺在主持开凿广通渠时，不是简单地疏浚汉代漕渠的河床，而是在原有河床的基础上统一规划航道，还在航道上设立保证运河水位的一系列闸坝，使这条运河可以通行拥有四个桅杆、四张大帆的巨船。这条运河的凿通，为后来隋朝大运河的兴建积累了宝贵的技术经验。

当时南朝最后一个政权陈还未被彻底消灭，为了实现全国的完全统一，隋文帝准备大举伐陈。587年，隋文帝下诏开凿山阳渎。山阳渎北起山阳（今江苏淮安），南至邗城（今江苏扬州），基本上就是春秋时吴国邗沟的故道。重新开凿这条运河一方面是为了保障伐陈战争的补给，另一方面也为将来的漕运准备好水上通道。山阳渎开通后，隋文帝在运河沿岸设置了几大粮食储运基地。漕运的兴盛使长安官仓内的粮食堆积如山，多达上千万石，布匹也有上千万匹。到了隋文帝末年，国家储备的物资可供

south, basically taking use of the old channel of the Hangou Canal built by the Wu State in the Spring and Autumn Period. The re-excavation of this canal not only guaranteed the supplies of the war against Chen, but also paved the water way to start the war from the River South Region. After the completion of the Shanyangdu Canal, the Emperor Wen of Sui set up several large food storage bases on the canal banks. The prosperous grain shipping piled up inexhaustible materials in Chang'an like mountains. By the late years of the Emperor Wen of Sui, the country's supplies in reserve could be used for 50 years. 20 years after the Tang Dynasty being established, the repertory in Chang'an was still not exhausted.

In 605, the Emperor Yang of Sui inherited the throne and moved the capital to Luoyang, which locates in the Central Plains and has admirable geographic position. As the Central Shaanxi Plain where Daxing City located was too narrow and small to bear the supplying of the capital, Luoyang with traffic convenience was better appropriate for the political and economic development at that time and could better stabilize the country. After ascending the seat, the Emperor Yang of Sui started preparing

50年之用，而长安的库存直到唐朝又用了20年仍未用完。

605年，隋炀帝登上皇位，并迁都洛阳。洛阳地处中原，地理位置上具有驾驭全国的气势，同时又因大兴城所处的关中平原狭小闭塞，当时已经难以负担对京师的供应，而迁都四通八达的洛阳正好符合当时的政治、经济发展趋势，更有利于稳定局势。即位之后，隋炀帝就准备以洛阳为中心开凿一条贯穿南北的大运河。

据史籍记载，隋朝大运河的开凿共分为三个阶段，首先开凿的是通济渠。通济渠起于洛阳西苑，利用东汉时的阳渠故道引谷、洛二水注入黄河，引汴水南下入淮河，越过淮河后接通山阳渎，到江都与长江相连。这条运河长达千余里，是一条负责北上南下、起着中枢作用的交通干线。通济渠河道宽广、水源充足、水深流缓，河岸上还有与运河平行的御道，道路两边栽种杨柳，景色极为壮观。

605年，隋炀帝征发民夫百余万，开始修凿通济渠。因为大量使用古运河的现成河道，所以这条千

to excavate a big canal running north and south basing in Luoyang.

According to history record, the excavation of the Grand Canal was divided into three stages. The first section be excavated was the Tongji Canal, which started from western Luoyang. The canal took use of the old channel of Yangqu Canal built in the Eastern Han Dynasty to direct the Gushui and Luoshui Rivers into the Yellow River. The canal also directed the Bianshui River heading south and passing through the Huaihe River to connect with the Shanyangdu Canal, and then run into the Yangtze River at Jiangdu. This canal is over 500 kilometers long and an important traffic artery, taking the responsibility of connecting the north and the south. The Tongji Canal has wide watercourse, abundant water source, deep water depth, and slow current. Meanwhile there is a royal road parallel to the canal on the bank. Along the road there grows willows, and the scenery is spectacular.

In 605, the Emperor Yang of Sui collected over a million of people to excavate the Tongji Canal. As vast of ready-made old canals could be taken use of, the completion of the project only took 155 days. The Tongji Canal is around

• 淡绿釉四系瓷罐（隋）
Light Green Glazed Porcelain Jar with Four Handles (Sui Dynasty, 581-618)

里长河只用了155天即告竣工。通济渠河宽60—80米、水深4米，不仅在漕运方面起着重要作用，而且还具备引水、蓄水、分洪、灌溉、绿化和改良两岸土壤等功能。为了庆祝这条运河的通航，隋炀帝举行了极大规模的庆祝仪式。在向新渠引水的同时，隋炀帝又下诏建造龙舟，组成一支庞大的船队。其中，最大的龙舟长66.7米，宽10米，高15米，船上有四层建筑，120个房间。最上一层造有三间大殿，殿上起楼，楼外有阁，处处雕栏彩绘，以珠玉和

60 meters wide and 4 meters deep, not only played an important role in the grain transportation field, but also possessed functions of river diversion, impoundment, flood diversion, irrigation, afforestation and soil reclamation. To celebrate the completion of this canal, the Emperor Yang of Sui held a large-scale celebration, and built a huge fleet of dragon boats. Among which, the largest dragon boat was 20 *Zhang* (a unit of length, 1 *Zhang* equal to 3.33 meters) long, 3 *Zhang* wide and 4.5 *Zhang* high, and equipped with four layer building and 120 rooms. The top layer had three audience halls, which were equipped with towers and attics, and decorated with paintings, peals and jades, and colored silk curtains. The whole dragon boat was just like an imperial palace above water.

According to the historical record, on August 15th of the lunar calendar, 605, the Emperor Yang of Sui set off for Jiangdu (today's Yangzhou in Jiangsu Province). On August 18 of the lunar calendar, he arrived at the Yellow River through the Caoqu Canal and Luoshui River by a red boat, and changed to the huge royal dragon boat. The empress's boat was called Xiangchi boat, which was smaller than the dragon boat but same in the decoration. Besides, the fleet was also accompanied

五彩锦幕装饰，整个大船就像一座水上皇宫。

据史书记载，当年农历八月十五，隋炀帝动身巡视江都（今江苏扬州）。八月十八，隋炀帝乘坐红色的小船，从漕渠经洛水进入黄河，而后改乘大型的皇家龙舟。皇后所乘坐的叫做翔螭舟，规格比龙舟稍小，但装饰无异。另外船队还配有名为"浮景"的副船九艘。还

• 古书上关于隋炀帝乘龙舟巡游的插图
Illustration in Ancient Book About Emperor Yang of Sui Touring on Dragon Boat

with nine auxiliary boats called Fujing and thousands of other boats used by the emperor's harem, princes, marquises, princesses, ministers, monks, nuns and Taoists, and for carrying the tributes. Over 80 thousand boat trackers were employed to drag the boats and thousands of warships were accompanied with the fleet. The fleet stretched over 100 kilometers, and the lights from the fleet illuminated the river and banks at night, together with the cavalries going along with the fleet on the banks like the wings; the scenery was extremely awe-inspiring; the Emperor Yang of Sui and his dragon boat arrived at Jiangdu not until October.

In the second year after the completion of the Tongji Canal, vast grain was shipped to Luoyang due to the convenience of the canal. To store the grain, the Emperor Yang of Sui gave orders to build the Luokou Granary in Gongxian County to the east of Luoyang, and built castle around the granary to protect it. Meanwhile, 3000 basements were excavated, and each basement could store 8000 *Dan* (a unit of dry measure for grain) of grain. Besides, another granary called Huiluo Granary was built to the northwest of Luoyang, which had 300 basements. These two large storages

有漾副船数千艘，供后宫、诸王、公主、百官、僧、尼、道士等乘坐，以及用来装载各地进献的物品，一共动用了拉纤的民夫8万多人。船队中还有数千艘军舰随行。船队首尾相连，绵延二百余里，夜晚船上的灯火照耀水陆，岸上有骑兵像两翼一样护卫随行，旌旗蔽野。隋炀帝坐着龙舟直到十月份才到江都，一路上威风极了。

通济渠通航的第二年，由于漕运顺畅，漕粮被大量运至洛阳。为了储存这些粮食，隋炀帝下诏在洛阳以东的巩县修筑洛口仓，并在粮仓外筑城以进行保护，同时挖了3000个地窖，每窖都可以储存8000石粮食。洛阳西北方又建了一座方圆十里的回洛仓，这座仓城有地窖300个。洛阳城外的这两处大仓可储藏粮食300万石，成为洛阳的主要粮食供给保障。

608年，为了向北方用兵，隋炀帝又征集河北一带的民夫上百万人，开凿南起黄河、北至涿郡（今北京）的永济渠，全长两千余里。永济渠的开凿也利用了大量的天然河道和古运河。其南段河道是将黄

outside Luoyang could store three million *Dan* of grain and became the major guarantees of Luoyang.

In 608, to assault the north, the Emperor Yang of Sui once again gathered over million of people in Hebei Province to excavate the Yongji Canal, which started from the Yellow River in the south and ended in Zhuojun County (today's Beijing) in the north and was more than 1000 kilometers. The excavation of the Yongji Canal also adopted vast natural rivers and old canals. Its southern section was constructed based on the natural Qinshui River, the tributary of the Yellow River, by widening, dredging and deepening processes, and connected with the Tongji Canal. Not like the Tongji Canal, which was applied for grain shipping, the excavation of the Yongji Canal was for military use. The Emperor Yang of Sui intended to start a massive war against Korea, and this canal was made to serve the war. In 611, the Yongji Canal was fully completed. The Emperor Yang of Sui toured north on the Yongji Canal by dragon boat, from Jiangdu to Zhuojun County, passing through the Huaihe River, Yellow River, Yongji Canal and Haihe River. During the tour, he comprehended the local conditions of

河支流沁水的天然河道拓宽、疏浚、加深而成,下与通济渠相连。与通济渠的漕运用途不同,隋炀帝开凿永济渠主要是为了军事用途,他想发动一场对高句丽的大

the people and the situation of the ethnic groups in the north in detail.

The last section the Grand Canal project was the 324 kilometers long Jiangnan Canal, the water artery connecting

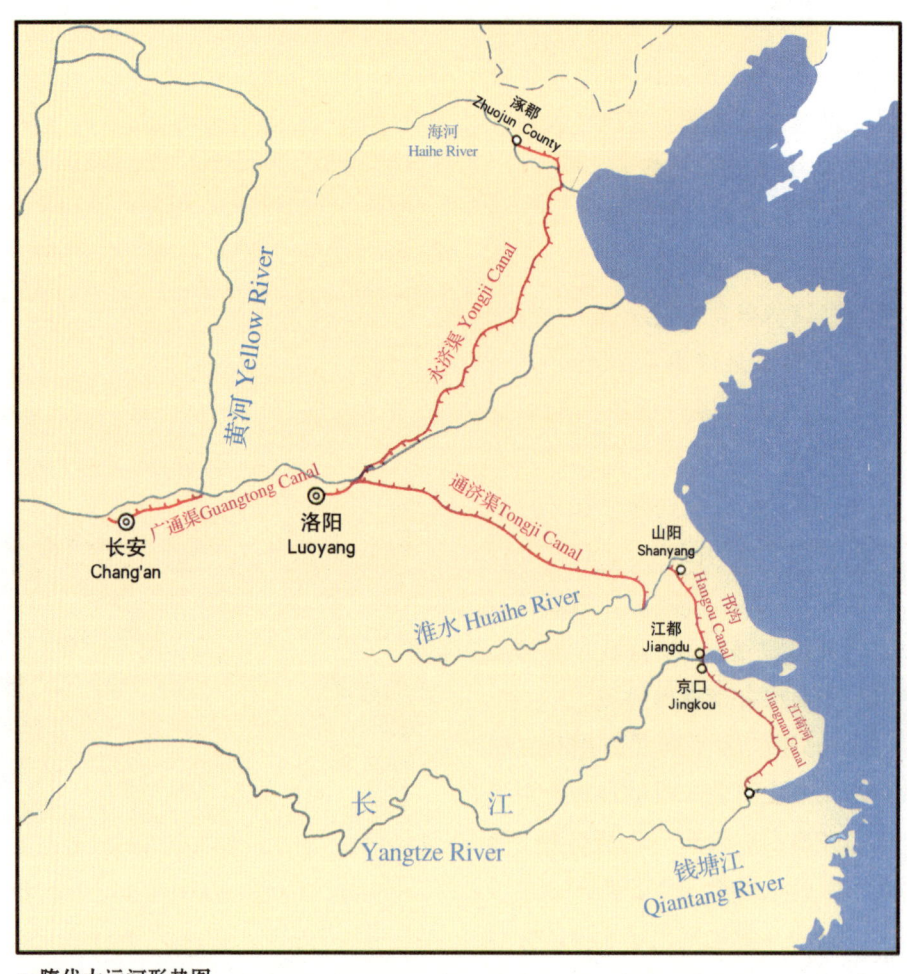

隋代大运河形势图
Map of the Grand Canal in the Sui Dynasty

规模战争，这条运河便是为这场战争服务的。611年，永济渠全线竣工。隋炀帝乘龙舟顺着永济渠北上巡视，从江都穿过淮河、黄河，进入永济渠，再经过海河，一直到达涿郡。巡游中，他还详细了解了当地的民情和北部少数民族的情况。

隋朝大运河的最后一段工程是全长324千米的江南河，这是一条将富庶的江南同北方相连的水运干线。它起自长江南岸的京口，经云阳、毗陵、过吴郡、嘉兴最终到达杭州。江南河宽33.3米，深3.3米，比通济渠和永济渠的规模小得多，但它的开凿意义非凡，历史上延续一千多年的南粮北运便是从江南河的竣工时开始的。

据史籍记载，从大业元年（605年）起的五年内，隋炀帝几乎同时开展三项大的工程，包括营建东都洛阳、修筑长城和开凿大运河，共征发民工600多万人次，给百姓造成了极其沉重的负担。在施工过程中，由于工期紧、劳动量大，民工死伤无数。据统计，仅开凿运河一项就死了200万人，再加上隋炀帝穷

the wealthy southern regions and the north. The canal starts from Jingkou on the southern bank of the Yangtze River to Hangzhou, passing through Yunyang, Piling, Wujun County and Jiaxing. The Jiangnan Canal is 10 *Zhang* (a unit of length, 1 *Zhang* equal to 3.33 meters) wide and 1 *Zhang* deep, much smaller than the scale of the Tongji Canal and the Yongji Canal. But the importance of its excavation is significant. The transport of the grain from Southern China to the north has over a thousand years of history, and just started from the completion of the Jiangnan Canal.

According to the historical record, from 605 to 610, the Emperor Yang of Sui carried out three large projects practically at the same time, including constructing the east capital Luoyang, building the Great Wall and excavating the Grand Canal. As over 6 million workers were levied in total, the people suffered privation and myriad hardships. During the construction, countless workers died of harsh time limitation and heavy work. According to the statistics, merely the excavation of the Grand Canal caused 2 million deaths. Meanwhile, as wantonly engaging in military aggression and extorting excessive taxes and levies, the

● 洛阳龙门石窟远眺
Distant View of Longmen Grottoes in Luoyang

兵黩武、横征暴敛，终于引起了各地百姓的反抗。618年，隋炀帝在江都宫中被叛将所杀，隋王朝也随之灭亡了。

Emperor Yang of Sui encountered revolt from people all over the country. In 618, the Emperor Yang of Sui was killed in his Jiangdu Palace by a betrayer, and the Sui Dynasty perished subsequently.

## > 唐宋大运河的繁荣

隋代大运河的贯通，真正获得好处的是唐、宋两朝。因为隋朝已经将以洛阳为中心的运河网构筑起来，所以唐代没有像隋代那样大规模地开凿运河，而是对隋代遗留下来的运河加以疏浚、整治、补缀、扩建。

隋朝灭亡后，唐高祖又将都城设在长安。随着唐中央政权的巩固，机构逐步扩大，人数迅速膨胀。政府需要比以往多十几倍甚至几十倍的粮食来应付如此庞大的开支。关中地区虽号称沃野，但土地有限，物产远远满足不了京师所需。若遇水旱之灾，只能依赖江南一带运来的粮食维持。从广通渠到通济渠，中间要经过黄河。而黄河的这段河道要经过险峻的三门峡，

## > Prosperity of the Grand Canal in the Tang and Song Dynasties

The cutthrough of the Grand Canal by the Sui Dynasty benefited the subsequent Tang and Song dynasties. As the Sui Dynasty had already constructed the Luoyang-based canal systems, the Tang Dynasty didn't see massively-excavated canals like the Sui Dynasty, but dredged, cleared-up, patched and expanded canals reserved from the Sui Dynasty.

After the perishing of the Sui Dynasty, the First Emperor of Tang once again chose Chang'an as capital. As the central government of Tang gradually being consolidated, the organizations expanded day by day, and the rapid expansion of the population, the government needed much more grain to solve the huge expenditure.

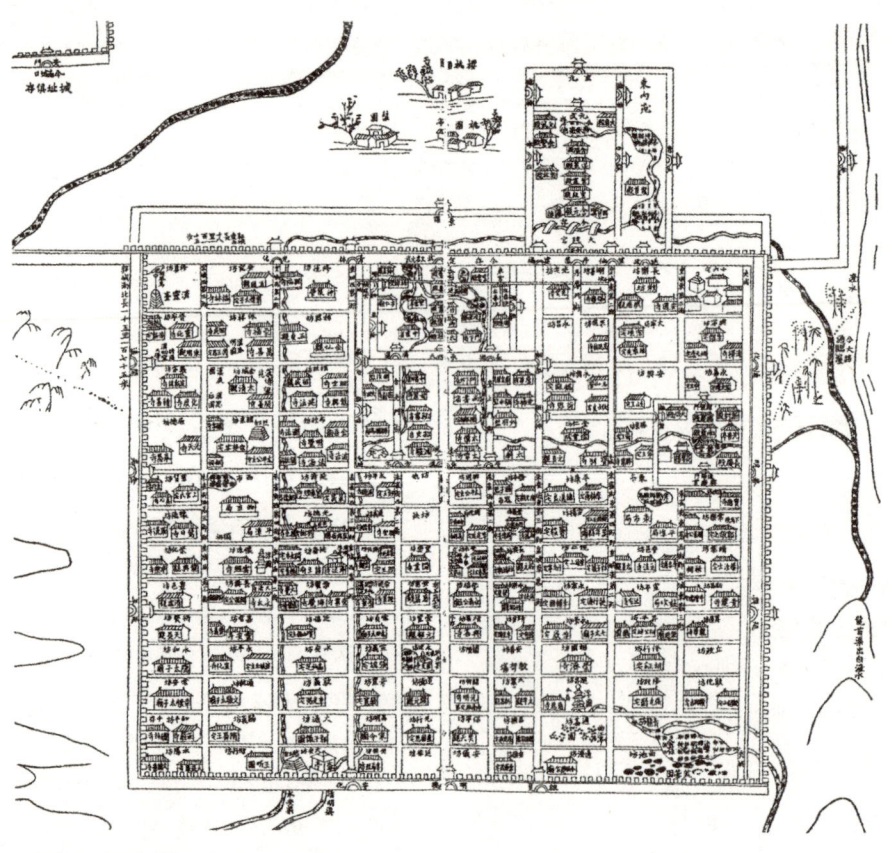

- **唐代长安城区域分布图（清人绘）**

  唐代都城长安面积达84平方千米，城内布局有如方整的棋盘，一座座外城墙将宫城层层包围，重重殿宇金碧辉煌。笔直的街道、整齐划一的居民区、四通八达的水运网络，体现了城市建设规划的周密、全面。

  **Regional Distribution Map of Chang'an in the Tang Dynasty (Produced in the Qing Dynasty)**

  Chang'an, the capital city of the Tang Dynasty, was 84 square kilometers in area. The distribution of the city was like an orderly chessboard, layers of defensive walls surrounded the resplendent and magnificent palaces. The straight streets, tidy residential quarters and water transport network extending in all directions presented the elaborate urban planning.

---

这里两岸夹水，壁立千仞，河心有两座石岛把河水分成三股，堪称天险。船只经过此地时即使格外小心，也很容易倾覆。由于三门峡的

Although the Central Shaanxi Plain had fertile soil, the land was too limited to satisfy the capital needs. When flood or drought occurred, the capital could only rely on the grain from the River South

阻碍，这一河段的水运量一直上不去，只能改走陆路。可是陆运的成本太高，效率也低，因此唐高宗、武则天、唐玄宗几位皇帝都曾多次带领官员前往洛阳，以解朝廷用度不足的窘况。

天宝三年（744年），唐玄宗下令整修广通渠。工程利用隋朝开凿的业已淤塞的广通渠旧河道，在

- **洪州窑褐绿釉团花纹茶碗（唐）**

  唐代制瓷业有了飞跃性的发展，而且唐代饮茶之风极盛，茶具之需剧增，为瓷器的发展注入了新活力。位于今江西南昌一带的洪州窑所产的各类茶具驰誉海内，不少精品都通过运河漕运进贡给唐王室。

  **Breen Glazed Regiment Flower Design Tea Bowl from Hongzhou Kiln (Tang Dynasty, 618-907)**

  The Tang Dynasty achieved huge development in the porcelain industry. Meanwhile as tasting tea had been popular all over the country, the need of tea sets was massively increased, injecting new vitality to the porcelain development. The Hongzhou Kiln near today's Nanchang in Jiangxi Province produced various kinds of world famous tea sets, many of the choicest among which were transported by ships to the royal court as tributes.

Region. From the Guangtong Canal to Tongji Canal, the Yellow River was the only way which must be passed, and the steep Sanmenxia Gorge lied right in this section of the Yellow River. As the river ran through the high cliffs and was cut by two rock islands in the middle of the river into three strands, the topography was extremely dangerous for shipping. Due to the blocking of the Sanmenxia Gorge, the cargo volume of this section had always been low, so the land route became the only option. But as the cost of the road transportation was too high and the efficiency was too low, the Emperor Gaozong, Empress Wu Zetian and Emperor Xuanzong of the Tang Dynasty all proceeded to Luoyang together with ministers for several times to solve the supply issues of the court.

In 744, the Emperor Xuanzong of Tang gave orders to repair the Guangtong Canal. The project took use of the foul Guangtong Canal excavated by the Sui Dynasty, created a channel paralleling with the Weishui River on its south. After entering the eastern section of the Weishui River from the Yellow River, ships could switch into this canal and directly reach Chang'an. This canal resolved the transportation problem of

渭水南边开辟了一条与渭水平行的河道，使运输船只从黄河开进渭水东段后折入这条运河，然后直达长安，从而解决了这段运输的麻烦，使长安与运河彻底连通起来。从此，长安真正成为唐王朝政治经济的中心。运河一直修到长安城城东的望春楼下，在那里挖了一个大湖，湖面宽广，可以停靠两三百艘大船，每艘船上都有一块木板写着船只的来历：有的船上写着来自广陵郡，并在甲板上陈列当地的织锦、铜器和海鲜；有的写着来自海南郡，船上陈列着南海的珍珠、玳

this section and thoroughly connected Chang'an to the canal. From then on, Chang'an truly became the economic and political center of the Tang Dynasty. The canal directly stretched to the Wangchun Tower in eastern Chang'an, where a large artificial lake that could take in over 300 ships was excavated. On each ship there was a board indicating the origin of the ship. The ships from Guangling County displayed the local brocades, bronze ware and seafood on the deck; some came from Hainan County and exhibited the pearls, hawksbill, ivories and agilawood from Hainan; some ships carried the paper and pens from Xuancheng County,

- **三彩胡人背猴骑驼俑（唐）**

  唐代的长安城堪称国际大都市，来到长安与唐通使的国家、地区多达300个，包括东罗马帝国、日本、阿拉伯帝国以及西域各国。波斯的珠宝，西域的良马、毛皮，西方的玻璃器皿等在长安街市上均可见到。

  **Three-color Glazed Figurine of a Foreigner with Monkey on His Back Riding a Camel (Tang Dynasty, 618-907)**

  Chang'an in the Tang Dynasty was an international metropolis, over 300 nations and regions including the Eastern Roman Empire, Japan, Arab Empire and Serindia countries had sent diplomatic envoys to Chang'an. Persian jewelry, fine horses and furs from the Western Regions, and Western glassware and so on could be found everywhere in Chang'an.

- **苏州枫桥**

枫桥位于苏州阊门外的枫桥镇，横跨于古运河山塘河段的枫桥湾上。这里是古代的水陆交通要道，设有护粮卡，漕粮北运经此时就封锁河道，禁止其他船只通行，故原名"封桥"，后改名"枫桥"。

**Fengqiao Bridge**

The Fengqiao Bridge locates in Fengqiao Town outside the Changmen Gate of Suzhou, stretching across the Fengqiao Bay, the Shantang Section of the ancient canal. This place was a land and water traffic artery in ancient times, and was set up with checkpoint. When there being a grain-ship passing, the other ships would be stopped to give way.

瑁、象牙、沉香；还有载着宣城郡的纸、笔，豫章郡的瓷器等各地特产的大船鱼贯从望春楼下驶过，绵延数里。可以说，是大运河造就了盛唐，大唐帝国也因此而成为世界瞩目的强国。

唐代宗时，宰相刘晏受命掌管

and some carried the porcelains produced in Yuzhang County. These ships sailed down the Wangchun Tower one by one, the fleet stretched for several miles. In a manner of speaking, the Grand Canal brought about the prosperity of the Tang Dynasty, made it a powerful nation of the world.

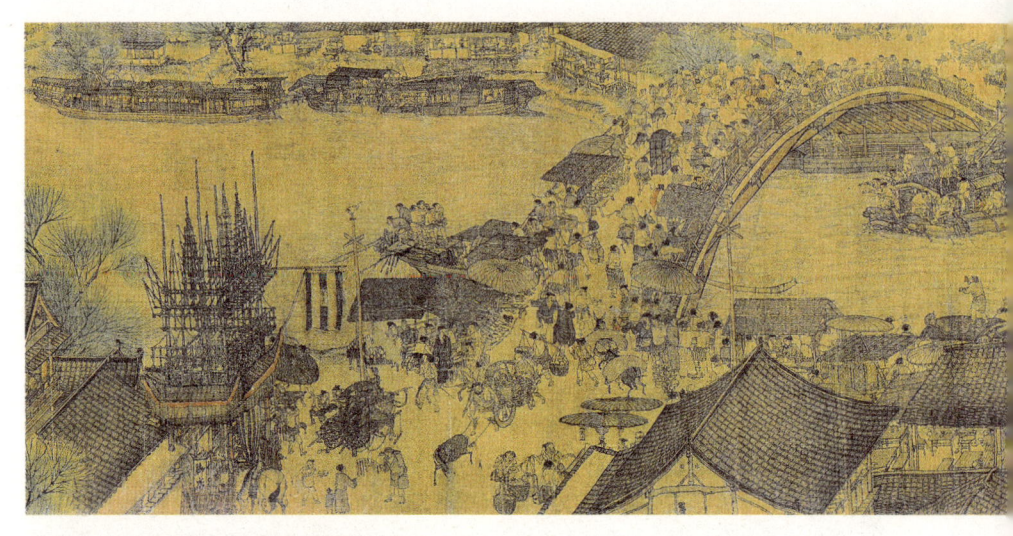

- **《清明上河图》【局部】张择端（北宋）**

  北宋时期，都城汴京不仅是全国水陆交通的中心，也是全国的商业中心。汴京繁华热闹的场景，被北宋画家张择端留在了著名的绘画长卷《清明上河图》中。画面中段的主题是繁忙的汴河码头，画面上人烟稠密、粮船云集。

  *Life along the Bian River at the Pure Brightness Festival* by Zhang Zeduan [Partial] (Northern Song Dynasty, 960-1127)

  During the Northern Song Dynasty, the capital Bianjing was not only the nationwide land and water communication center, but also the business center of the nation. The prosperous scenery was recorded by the court painter of the Northern Song Dynasty Zhang Zeduan in his masterpiece *Life along the Bian River at the Pure Brightness Festival*. The middle part of the work displays the busy Bianjiang wharf, which was crowded with people and grain-ships.

漕运。他根据各段运河的河道、地势、水势的不同特点，采取长江、汴河、黄河、渭水分段接运的办法，解决了各段河道水位、水势不

During the reign of the Emperor Dai Zong of Tang, the minister Liu Yan was dispatched to manage the grain shipping. Considering the various characters of the channels, topographies and water potentials of the different canal sections, he adopted the sectionalized successive transportation method breaking the Yangtze River, Bianhe Canal, Yellow River and Weishui River, resolved the continuous shipping issue due to the various water potentials and water levels of different sections. The court also built large storages at the interfaces of different sections as transfer stations. Meanwhile, Liu Yan aroused the masses living by the rivers to dredge the channels, maintain

同致使船只难以连续通行的问题。朝廷还在各段河道岸口建造大仓库，作为装卸储藏的转运站。刘晏又发动沿河民众疏浚河道，培护河堤，修筑船闸河堰。从此，运河各段河水长流，漕船如梭般穿行于运河之中。

北宋建都汴京（今河南开封），依然沿用隋代的运河系统。为开封提供漕运支持的运输干线是隋炀帝开凿的通济渠，在宋代被叫做"汴河"。这条运河的最前身是战国时魏惠王开凿的鸿沟，北宋时这条运河被视为国家的命脉。当时的汴河经过精心整修，整条河深浅

the levees and construct the locks and weirs. From then on, the grain-ships could easily transfer between various sections of canals.

The Northern Song Dynasty chose Bianjing (today's Kaifeng in Henan Province) as capital, and remained the canal system from the Sui Dynasty. The Tongji Canal excavated by the Emperor Yang of Sui was the transportation artery supporting the needs of Kaifeng, and was called the "Bianhe Canal" in the Song Dynasty. The predecessor of this canal was the Honggou Canal excavated by the King Hui of Wei in the Warring States Period. The Northern Song Dynasty considered this canal the lifeline of the country. The Bianhe Canal of that time was carefully maintained, the water level of the whole canal was well-proportioned and the water potential was gently. As the largest full load grain-ship in the Song Dynasty drafted around 1.3 meters, the Bianhe Canal was designed around 2 meters, and the riverbed was paved with flagstones. Every year, the sludge in the canal must be cleared to unfold the flagstones. Besides the management of the Bianhe Canal, Northern Song Dynasty also successively excavated the Wuzhang Canal (renamed "Guangji

• 开封开宝寺塔

开封开宝寺塔始建于北宋仁宗皇祐元年（1049年），是一座仿楼阁式的实心砖塔，因塔的外壁全部用深褐色琉璃面砖装饰，远看近似铁铸，被人们俗称为"铁塔"。

**Kaifeng Iron Pagoda**

The Kaifeng Iron Pagoda was firstly built in 1049 in the Northern Song Dynasty, is a pavilion-styled solid brick tower. As the tower cliff was built in dark brown glazed bricks and looks like iron from a distance, people commonly call it the Iron Pagoda.

均匀、水势平缓。当时最大的漕船满载时吃水1.3米，因此规定汴河水深2米，并在河床上埋下石人石板，每年都要清除一次河道里的淤泥，规定必须清理到石板为止。在重点经营汴河的同时，北宋还相继开凿了由汴京通往山东地区的五丈河（后称"广济河"），通往西南和南方的蔡河（后称"惠民河"），以及作为五丈河水源的金水河。黄河、汴渠、蔡河、五丈河共同构成了以汴京为中心的运河网络。宋太

Canal" later) stretching from Bianjing to Shandong region, the Caihe Canal (renamed "Huimin Canal" later) accessing to the south and west, and the Jinshui Canal, which was the water head of the Wuzhang Canal. The Yellow River, Bianhe Canal, Caihe Canal and Wuzhang Canal together constituted the Bianjing-based canal network. The Emperor Taizu of Song paid great attention to the canal projects and had interviewed the construction sites in person for several times. Meanwhile, the Northern Song Dynasty massively repaired the old Hangou Canal (also called the Chuyang Canal during the Song Dynasty) to assure the smooth traffic in the Yangtze-Huaihe Region. The govenment of the Song Dynasty also rebuilt the Lingqu Canal, and increased its delivery gates to improve the transport capacity, for

祖对运河工程十分重视，几次亲临施工地巡视。此外，为保障江淮地区的运道畅通，北宋政府还重点整治了邗沟故道（宋代又称楚扬运河）。为加强与岭南地区之间的联系，政府还重修了灵渠，增设斗门以提高运力。

北宋时期，不仅漕运中心由洛阳转移到开封，而且由于经济重心

enhancing the communication with the Lingnan Region.

During the Northern Song Dynasty, the grain shipping center moved from Luoyang to Kaifeng. Meanwhile, because the economic center gradually moved southward, the North-South Canal constituted by the Bianhe Canal, Hangou Canal and Jiangnan Canal was more and more important and became the economic

• 宋代漕船模型（图片提供：FOTOE）
Model of Grain-ship in the Song Dynasty

龙泉窑青瓷鬲式炉（南宋）
Celadon Furnace from Longquan Kiln
(Southern Song Dynasty, 1127-1279)

的逐渐南移，由汴河、邗沟、江南河构成的南北运河的地位日趋重要，成为北宋王朝的经济命脉。宋钦宗靖康二年（1127年），康王赵构在南京（今河南商丘）即位，后来又将国都迁到临安（今浙江杭州），建立了南宋。宋室的南迁使得大运河的南北交通暂时中断，但以临安为中心的区域性运河系统又重新生成。此时，江南运河成为南宋王朝的生命线。由于地势平坦、水源充足，江南运河是全国运河中水运条件最好的一段，自三国时东吴首开破冈渎以来，直到南宋一直保持畅通，从未荒废。当时江南运河沿岸的重镇杭州、嘉兴和湖州已经成为手工业最为发达的地区。这里不仅是著名的鱼米之乡、丝绸之

lifeline of the Northern Song Dynasty. In May of the 1127, Zhao Gou ascended the throne in Nanjing (today's Shangqiu in Henan Province), and later switched the capital to Lin'an (today's Hangzhou in Zhejiang Province) and established the Southern Song Dynasty. The migrating southward of Song shortly suspended the Grand Canal transportation, but soon later the Lin'an based regional canal system was took into use. At this moment, the Jiangnan Canal became the lifeline of the Southern Song Dynasty. Because of the level topography and plentiful water, the Jiangnan Canal possessed the best water transportation condition of the country, and had always been expediting since its completion in the Three Kingdoms Period. The handicrafts industry of the major towns by the Jiangnan Canal including Hangzhou, Jiaxing and Huzhou was mostly developed. The region was not only the famous as "Land of Honey

府，而且是人文荟萃的文化之都，这一切都有力地支撑了南宋王朝的统治。

and Milk" and "Land of Silk", but also the state of talents, powerfully supporting the reign of the Southern Song Dynasty.

### 宋徽宗的花石纲

宋徽宗赵佶是个有名的艺术家，在书法、绘画、诗歌方面都卓有成就，然而在政治上昏庸无能，生活上骄奢。他酷爱收藏花石，于是有官员专门索求奇花异石，以船运往东京进贡。当时江浙一带凡是平民家中有一木一石、一花一草可供玩赏

- 北宋花石纲遗物——苏州留园冠云峰
  Flower-stone *Gang* Relic of the Northern Song Dynasty—Cloud Capped Peak in Lingering Garden in Suzhou

的，应奉局立即派人以黄纸封之，征为供奉皇帝之物，搬运时则破墙拆屋而去。这些运送花石的船只每十船编为一"纲"，从江南到东京，沿淮河、汴河而上，舳舻相接，络绎不绝，称为"花石纲"。为保障花石纲的运输，关系国家民生的漕运都被挤在一边，漕船和大量商船都被强征来运送花石。花石纲给东南地区百姓造成了极大的灾难，也成为激起各地民众起义造反的重要原因之一。

## Flower-stone *Gang* by Emperor Hui Zong of Song

Zhao Ji, the Emperor Hui Zong of Song and the famous emperor of art, achieved great accomplishments in calligraphy, painting and poesy, but was fatuous in politics and lapped in luxury. He ardently loved collecting flowers and stones. Some ministers specially sought for exotic flowers and stone for him and shipped them to the capital. At that time, if a family in Jiangsu or Zhejiang regions possessed unusual flowers or stones, the Tribute Bureau would immediately carry it off and send to the emperor as tribute. The ships transporting the flowers and stones were grouped 10 ships a *Gang*. The ships sailed from the River South Region to the capital by the Huaihe River and Bianhe Canal in an endless stream, called the "Flower-stone *Gang*". The grain shipping was neglected, and many grain-ships and merchant ships were impressed, to guarantee the Flower-stone *Gang* shipping, which brought miserable life to the people in southeast China, and was one of the major reasons of the rebels spreading all over the country.

## > 元代大运河的定型

继秦始皇和隋文帝之后，忽必烈在历史上第三次完成了对中国的统一，结束了自唐中期开始的天下割据的局面，为元、明、清三代600多年的统一局面奠定了基础。元世祖忽必烈在隋炀帝之后第二次开凿贯穿中国南北的大运河——京杭大运河，使北方的政治中心与江南的经济重镇连成一体，为元朝以及后来的统治者又一次修造了这条贯通五大水系的水运大动脉。

1271年，元朝定都大都（北京），运河发展进入一个新的历史阶段。元初，北宋时十分繁荣的汴河早已淤塞，永济渠只有部分河段通航，所以漕运只能采取水陆联运的方式，即走一段水路再上岸走陆路，然后再走水路，反复多次才能

## > Finalization of the Grand Canal in the Yuan Dynasty

After the First Emperor of Qin and Emperor Wen of Sui, the Kublai Khan unified China for the third time, which terminated the secession from the middle Tang Dynasty to the Song Dynasty, and laid the foundation for the over 600 years' unity of the Yuan, Ming and Qing dynasties. Kublai Khan excavated the north-south Beijing-Hangzhou Grand Canal, connecting the political center in north China with the economic towns in River South Region together. After the construcuction of the Grand Canal by Emperor Yang of Sui, the Kublai Khan built as well as repairing this water traffic artery, which connected the five major water systems, once again for the Yuan Dynasty and the subsequent rulers.

In 1271, Dadu (Beijing) was chosen as capital of the Yuan Dynasty, and

通州古运河河道 (摄影：陈闻达)
Channel of Ancient Canal in Tongzhou

将漕粮从江南运至大都。这种方式运输效率极低、成本又高，一年的漕运量不过30万石。为了满足朝廷的需要，南方的漕粮往往只能采用海运的方式运至北方。但是海上运输风险较大，每年都有漕船在海上倾覆，常常造成数十万石漕粮漂浮海上、数千漕卒溺水而死的悲剧。为彻底解决南粮北运的问题，元朝廷对隋唐大运河进行了一次大规模的整治和开发。

the development of canal accordingly stepped into a new historic stage. At the beginning of the Yuan Dynasty, the prosperous Bianhe Canal left from the Northern Song Dynasty had been silted up and the only partial sections of the Yongji Canal could be used for shipping. As a result, the grain shipped from the River South Region to Dadu could only adopt water-land transshipment mode, which was low in efficiency and high in cost, the transportation volume per year was only three hundred thousand *Dan* (a unit of dry measure for grain). To meet the needs of the court, usually the grain in the south had to be shipped to the north by sea. But the risk of sea transportation was unpredictable. Every year there were grain-ships capsized in the sea, causing hundreds of thousands of grain's loss and thousands of soldiers' dead. To completely resolve the south-north grain shipping issue, the Yuan Dynasty massively repaired and developed the Grand Canal built by the Sui Dynasty.

In 1276, Guo Shoujing, the famous scientist in the Yuan Dynasty, surveyed the topography in Hebei and Shandong provinces and planned the course of the canal. He left from Beijing for south, surveyed the canal topography on foot,

1276年，元代著名科学家郭守敬去河北、山东一带勘察地形，规划运河路线。他从北京出发，一路向南步行调查、勘测运河地形，与另一位水利专家马之贞制定了整治大运河的方针。1280年，朝廷采纳马之贞的建议，动工开凿济州（今济宁市）至东平安山的济州河，全长75千米。1289年，元世祖忽必烈下诏令马之贞主持开凿起于须城（今山东东平）安山西南到临清的一段运河，征调民夫250多万人。半年后，运河竣工。忽必烈

and drafted the Grand Canal dredging policy together with another hydraulician Ma Zhizhen. In 1280, the court adopted Ma Zhizhen's suggestion and started to excavate 75 kilometers long Jizhou Canal from Jizhou (today's Jining in Shandong Province) to Anshan Mountain in Dongping. In 1289, the Kublai Khan ordered Ma Zhizhen to manage the canal project excavating from southwest Anshan Mountain in Xucheng (today's Dongping in Shandong Province) to Linqing, over 2.5 million civilian workers were called up. Half a year later, the canal was completed and named the "Huitong Canal" by the Kublai Khan. Huitong Canal was 125 kilometers long, and the topography was extremely complex and rarely water sources were available within the region, the construction required very high project technology. As this section of canal possessed the most ship locks among all the sections, people praised it as the "Canal of Lock".

Before the excavation of the Beijing-Hangzhou Grand Canal, the grain

● 郭守敬像
Portrait of Guo Shoujing

## 科学家郭守敬

郭守敬（1231—1316）是中国元代的天文学家、数学家、水利学家和仪器制造家。他与王恂等人共同编制的《授时历》是中国古代历法发展到巅峰状态的标志。郭守敬一生先后设计制作的天文仪器约有12种，包括简仪、仰仪、玲珑仪等。这些仪器不仅结构新颖，而且实用有效。郭守敬还主持进行了大量的天文观测工作，包括恒星位置、冬至时刻、回归年长度、五星近日点黄经等。晚年，郭守敬致力于河工水利，提出并完成了自大都到通州的运河(即白浮堰和通惠河)工程。

## Scientist Guo Shoujing

Guo Shoujing (1231-1316) was the astronomer, mathematician, hydraulician, and instrument maker in the Yuan Dynasty of China. The *Shoushi Calendar* compiled by him and Wang Xun marks the peak of Chinese ancient calendar. Guo Shoujing had made about 12 kinds of astronomical instruments in his life, including abridged armilla, upward-looking bowl sundial and so on, which were not only original in structure, but also practical and efficient. Guo Shoujing also directed vast astronomical observation works, including the study of the star apparent place, winter solstice time, solar year length, five-star perihelion longitude and so on. In his later years, Guo Shoujing devoted himself to the water conservancy project, proposed and completed the canal from Dadu to Tongzhou (Baifu Weir and Tonghui Canal).

• 郭守敬制造的简仪复原模型
Recovered Model of Abridged Armilla Made by Guo Shoujing

将这条运河定名为"会通河"，会通河经过地段的地形极其复杂，当地又缺少水源，因此工程技术要求非常高，水闸设置是所有河段中最多的，以至百姓将其称为"闸河"。

　　京杭大运河开凿之前，漕粮运至通州后上岸，再从陆路运往大都。每逢秋季漕粮运来时，恰逢北京进入雨季，道路泥泞，死在运粮路上的驴子不计其数。至元二十九年（1292年），元世祖忽必烈决定将郭守敬早就提出的开凿御河的建议付诸实施。郭守敬引白浮山泉为水源，御河起自昌平县白浮村，过双塔、榆河、一亩、玉泉等河流再由西向东入大都城，之后向南经积水潭，东南出文明门至通州注入白河，总长82千米。对于这条贯穿京师的御河，元世祖非常重视。施工期间，他亲自命令朝廷自丞相以下所有大臣都要去运河工地参与搬运土石，以为百姓表率。御河通航后，元世祖见到积水潭湖面船帆林立，军民正在忙碌地装卸漕粮的景象，非常高兴，当即为御河赐名"通惠河"。通惠河的开通使漕运

arriving at Tongzhou by ship should be transferred onto land vehicles, and then transported to Dadu. When autumn, the harvest season came, Beijing was in the rainy season, causing countless donkeys to die on the muddy grain shipping road. By 1292, the Kublai Khan decided to carry out the excavation plan of the royal canal early proposed by Guo Shoujing. Guo Shoujing directed the spring from Baifu Mountain as the river source of the royal canal, and constructed the canal from Baifu Village in Changping County. The canal flew east through the rivers of Shuangta, Yuhe, Yimu and Yuquan to the downtown of Dadu, then turned south and flew through the Jishui Pool, and at last flew southeast out of the Wenming Gate to Tongzhou and entered into the Baihe River. The overall length of the canal was 82 kilometers. The Kublai Khan particularly valued this royal canal which ran through the capital. During the construction period, he ordered all ministers except the prime ministers to participate in the construction as examples to common people. After the completion of the royal canal, the Kublai Khan was glad to see the prosperous view of the grain handling scene by the Jishui Pool and immediately gave it the

青瓷舟形砚滴（元）
Celadon Boat Shaped *Yandi* (a Small Container of Water for Inkstone) (Yuan Dynasty, 1206-1368)

效率立即改观，年漕运量很快上升至100万石。如此巨大的运输量，使得从通州到天津原有的隋唐时期的永济渠已经难以应付。于是，在通惠河凿通一年后，元世祖又开工程为通州运粮河注入水源。

至此，全长近1800千米的京杭大运河全部完成。整条运河由七个部分组成：从北京到通州全长164里的通惠河，从通州向南连通大沽河的通州粮河，从天津向南至山东临清、连接通州粮河与会通河的卫河，从临清至须城的会通河，从须城连通泗水的济州河，连通淮河与长江的扬州运河（隋文帝开凿的

name "Tonghui Canal". The completion of the Tonghui Canal improved the grain shipping efficiency at once, and the shipping volume per year rose to a million *Dan*. As the old Tongzhou-Tianjin Yongji Canal built by the Sui and Tang dynasties couldn't bear such huge shipping volume, the Kublai Khan started another project to add new water source to the Tongzhou Grain Canal.

By then, the 1750 kilometers long Beijing-Hangzhou Grand Canal was fully completed. The whole canal was constituted of seven sections, including the 82 kilometers long Tonghui Canal from Beijing to Tongzhou, the Tongzhou Grain Canal from Tongzhou to Dagu River in the south, the Huitong Canal from Linqing to Xucheng, the Jizhou Canal from Xucheng to Sishui, the Yangzhou Canal (Shanyang Canal excavated by the Emperor Yang of Sui) connecting the Huaihe River and Yangtze River, and the Jiangnan Canal from Zhenjiang directly to Hangzhou. No longer based on Luoyang, the Grand Canal of the Yuan Dynasty started from Dadu, passing through

山阳渎），从镇江直达杭州的江南运河。元代大运河不再绕道洛阳，而是从大都起，直穿山东、江苏全境，径抵江南，把南北方各大经济区更直接地联系起来，这是运河水道的又一次重大改变。

Shandong and Jiangsu provinces, to the River South Region. The canal possessed shorter cruising range and connected various major economic zones all over the country together in a more direct manner. It can be referred to as another rebirth of the canal.

- 元代北京漕运壁画，北京元大都城垣遗址公园
（图片提供：FOTOE）
Grain Shipping Mural in Beijing of the Yuan Dynasty, Yuan Dynasty City Wall Relics Park in Beijing

## 马可·波罗笔下的大运河

意大利人马可·波罗于1254年出生于威尼斯的一个商人家庭。1271年，17岁的他跟随父亲和叔叔去东方，1275年到达了元朝的上都（位于今内蒙古多伦县西北）。他们受到了元世祖忽必烈的接见。马可·波罗还留在元朝当官任职，在中国居留了17年。其间，马可·波罗曾多次前往中国东部和江南各地旅行。他在《马可·波罗游记》一书中这样描述当时的京杭大运河："这条交通线，是由许多河流、湖泊，以及一条又宽又深的运河组成的。这条运河，是根据大汗的旨意挖掘

的，其目的在于使用船只能够从一条大河转入另一条大河……直达汗八里（指元大都），不必取道于海。"他对大运河的终点——风景秀丽、商业繁华、交通便利的杭州城更是赞不绝口："这座城市的庄严和秀丽，堪为世界其他城市之冠。这里名胜古迹非常之多，使人们想象自己仿佛生活在天堂，所以有'天城'之名。"

## Grand Canal Mentioned by Marco Polo

The Italian Marco Polo was born in a Venetian merchant family in 1254. In 1271, the 17 year-old Marco followed his father and uncle to the East. When arriving at Shangdu (northwest to today's Duolun County in Inner Mongolia) in 1275, they were received by the Kublai Khan. Marco Polo resided in China for 17 years as an officer of the Yua Dynasty. During this period, he traveled to the eastern China and the River South Region for several times. Marco Polo mentioned the Beijing-Hangzhou Grand Canal of that time in his book, *Marco Polo's Travel Stories*, "This traffic line was constituted of many rivers, lakes and a deep wide canal, which was excavated according to the Khan's command in order to enable ships to transfer from one river to another, for the convenience of the transportation from the southern provinces to the capital and avoiding the ocean shipping." He also praised the beautiful, prosperous and traffic convenient Hangzhou, the terminal city of the Grand Canal, "It's the most dignified and beautiful city of the world. The scenic spots and historical sites spreading all over the city gave it the name of 'Heaven'."

• 马可·波罗的旅程
Journey of Marco Polo

> ## 明代大运河的维护

像唐王朝一样，明朝同样坐享前朝开河之利，开创了另一个漕运的鼎盛时期。

1368年朱元璋定都应天（今江苏南京）后，漕运更是四通八达，江西、湖广等地的军粮由长江直下，江苏一带的粮食由运河输送，供应陕西等地的粮食则从河南顺黄河逆流而上，转渭河西运。而都城南京所需的漕粮当时主要取自浙江和苏南地区。1393年，朱元璋下令开凿溧水胭脂河。这条运河位于南京南郊的溧水县城西部，全长7500米，沟通了溧水石臼湖与秦淮河上游的沙河口。运河凿通后，粮船便可从太湖经内陆直达南京，运输效率大大提高。

1403年，驻守北平的燕王朱棣

> ## Maintenance of the Grand Canal in the Ming Dynasty

Like the Tang Dynasty, the Ming Dynasty also fed on the fruits of the predecessor's labor and created another golden age of grain shipping.

After Zhu Yuanzhang chose Yingtian (today's Nanjing in Jiangsu Province) as capital in 1368, the grain shipping became much more convenient. The grain for the army produced in Jiangxi, Hubei and Hunan provinces could be shipped downstream through the Yangtze River; grain in Jiangsu Province was shipped out by canal; grain supplying Shaanxi Province was shipped out of Henan Province upstream the Yellow River, and then transferred to the Weihe River to the west. Meanwhile, the grain required by the capital Nanjing was mainly derived from Zhejiang and South Jiangsu regions. In 1393, Zhu Yuanzhang gave orders to

● 明太祖孝陵神道边的武将石像
Stone Statues of Generals Along the Sacred Way in Front of the Mausoleum of the First Emperor of the Ming Dynasty

率领军队攻入南京，夺取了皇位，改年号为永乐，他就是明成祖。1421年，明成祖迁都北京。随着明王朝的政治中心转移到北方，朝廷的漕运结构也发生了大规模变动。要将北京与江南经济中心连接起来，漕运是必不可少的手段。当时，元代的京杭大运河已多处淤塞，明成祖最初只能用海陆联运的方式运输漕粮。但海运风险很大，每年要损失三分之一的漕粮。同时在北京建造皇宫所需的高档砖瓦、

excavate the Rouge River, which locates to the west of Lishui County in southern suburbs of Nanjing and is 7.5 kilometers long. This canal connected the Shijiu Lake in Lishui and Shahekou in the upstream areas of the Qinhuai River. The completion of the canal enabled grainships from the Taihu Lake region to directly reach Nanjing, greatly enhancing the transport efficiency.

In 1403, Zhu Di, garrisoning in Beijing, led his army occupying Nanjing and seized the throne. After renaming the reign title to Yong-le, Zhu Di became

珍稀木材只有南方才有，而且为了控制江南地区，必须能够快速地出动军队，因此重开贯穿南北的内河漕运迫在眉睫。

明成祖开凿京杭大运河的第一项工程便是重开会通河。1391年黄

the Emperor Chengzu of the Ming Dynasty. In 1406, the Emperor Chengzu of Ming switched the capital to Beijing. Together with the northward move of the regime's political center, the court's grain shipping structure also largely changed. The grain shipping was essential approach to connect Beijing and the River South economic center. However, as the Beijing-Hangzhou Grand Canal constructed in Yuan Dynasty had been silted up in many sections, the Emperor Chengzu of Ming could only adopt sea-land transportation manner for grain shipping at first. Average one third of the grain was lost in the transportation per year due to the high risk of ocean shipping. Meanwhile as the high-class tiles and precious woods needed for the construction of the palaces in Beijing were only produced in South China and for the controlling of the River South Region, the rebuilding of the north-south grain shipping was extremely urgent.

The first project operated by the Emperor Chengzu of Ming was the

- 南京溧水胭脂河天生桥（图片提供：FOTOE）
Natural Bridge Crossing Rouge River in Lishui, Nanjing

• 《天工开物》中的明代漕船图
Picture of Grain-Ship in the Ming Dynasty in *Exploitation of the Works of Nature*

河曾在山东境内决口，洪水过后，山东境内的会通河和济州河基本上被黄河带来的泥沙淤平。而会通河和济州河是整条京杭大运河的关键河段，只要将它们凿通，再加上通往长江的扬淮运河，基本上就可以实现漕粮的内河运输，从而废除费时、费力、高风险的海陆运输了。永乐八年（1410年）明成祖下旨重开会通河，当时征调民夫16.5万人，清理挖掘河道192.5千米。当时从河道中挖出的泥沙在运河附近推起了一座龙山，至今在龙山上还能看到当年栽种的松柏。竣工后，朝廷将元朝时开凿的会通河和济州河统称为"会通河"。

reconstruction of the Huitong Canal. The Yellow River used to breach in Shandong Province in 1391, and Huitong Canal and Jizhou Canal were basically filled up by the sediment carried by the flood. The Huitong and Jizhou Canals were critical sections of the whole Beijing-Hangzhou Grand Canal. As long as dredging them up, together with the Yanghuai Canal connecting with the Yangtze River, the grain shipping through inland waterway transportation instead of the time-consuming, arduous and high-risk sea-land transportation could be basically realized. The Emperor Chengzu of Ming gave orders to reconstruct the Huitong Canal in 1410. 160,000 civilian workers were mustered and over 190 kilometers of channel were cleared up. The sediment excavated from the channel was piled up into the Longshan Mountain, and the pine trees planted during that time can still be seen on the mountain till now. After the completion, the royal court jointed together the canals of Huitong and Jizhou excavated by the Yuan Dynasty and called it the Huitong Canal in general.

In the meantime of the reconstruction of the Huitong Canal, the Emperor Chengzu of Ming took 15 years to fully bore through the around 1800 kilometers

明成祖在集中力量重开会通河后，又用了15年的时间，把近1800千米长的京杭大运河全线凿通，将这条大运河凿成了一条河道又宽又深，航运设施非常完备的内河航线。明朝中叶，虽然黄河数次决口泛滥，洪水和泥沙数次中断了山东和苏北的漕运通道，但在朝廷的积极治理下，漕运依然保持了顺畅。正统年间，黄河在荥阳决口，洪水波及运河，使漕运中断。一位名叫徐有贞的治河能人向朝廷建议设置

long Beijing-Hangzhou Grand Canal, made it a inland ship route with deep wide channel and extensive shipping facilities. During the middle Ming Dynasty, the Yellow River breached for several times, and the flood and sediment repeatedly cut down the grain shipping in Shandong and north Jiangsu provinces, but the court actively managed to maintain the smooth of the shipping. During 1436 to 1449, the Yellow River breached in Xingyang and the flood suspended the grain shipping. A talent hydraulic expert called Xu Youzhen stood out, who suggested the court to set up sluice to split the flood, in order to assure the grain shipping. The Emperor Daizong of Ming supported his

- 明代船只复原模型
  Recovered Model of Ships in the Ming Dynasty

水闸，开河分流洪水，保证漕运。明代宗非常支持徐有贞的建议，命他主持维护工程。经过三年的努力，徐有贞在黄河决口处开凿出了一条新运河，并设置了水闸。明代宗大为高兴，为新渠赐名"广济渠"，将水闸命名"通源闸"。徐有贞的治理工程保证了运河30年的稳定。

明末，黄河再次决口，毁坏运河。然而这时的朝廷腐败，各机构运转不灵，整治运河漕运的效率越来越低。而且维护运河是一项耗费极大的工程，自明朝中期以后，朝廷的财政收入每况愈下，以至于入不敷出。在财政日益捉襟见肘的时候，明王朝只能压缩其他开支，维持向大运河拨款。嘉靖四十四年（1565年），黄河在江苏沛县决口，淤塞运河50千米。洪水过后，运河河道已经被泥沙填平，朝廷只能重新挖掘了一段新河道，绕过洪水区，以维持漕运。

suggestion and dispatched him to manage the maintenance project. After three years' endeavor, Xu Youzhen excavated a new canal equipped with sluice at the breach of the Yellow River. The Emperor Daizong was pleased by the project. He named the new canal Guangji Canal, and gave the sluice the name of Tongyuan Sluice. The controlling work of Xu Youzhen stabilized the canal for 30 years.

By the late Ming Dynasty, the Yellow River breached once again and ruined the canal. However for the corruption of the court during that period and the ineffective operation of the government bodies, the efficiency of canal shipping maintenance dropped lower day by day. Meanwhile as the canal maintenance project cost much, and the state revenue had been worse and worse since the middle Ming Dynasty, usually the court had to compress other expenditures to support the canal. In 1565, the Yellow River breached in Peixian County in Jiangsu Province and blocked the canal for over 50 kilomemers. As the channel had been filled and leveled up by the sediment after the flood, the court had no choice but to excavate a new section bypass the flood zone to maintain the grain shipping.

## 大运河古沉船

　　1999年，安徽淮北市的大运河故道边出土了8艘唐代沉船。在考古发掘中还发现了唐宋时期20多个窑口的精美瓷器以及陶器、砚台等各种文物。2012年4月，在北运河整治清淤改造施工过程中，人们在天津市北辰区张湾村的运河古河道发现了3艘明代沉船。经过考古人员的发掘，共出土元、明、清时期的铜、铁、瓷、陶、骨、木、竹等不同质地的文物及标本近千件。根据沉船的尺寸、形制和船上所载物资推断，该船可能为明代内河漕运中浅船的一种——剥船。这些古沉船见证了大运河上千年的发展与兴衰，也是研究漕运史和船舶史的珍贵资料。

## Ancient Sunken Ships in Grand Canal

In 1999, 8 sunken ships of the Tang Dynasty were excavated from the ancient channel of the Grand Canal in Huaibei, Anhui Province, together with fine cultural relics including porcelains, potteries, inkstones and so on produced in over 20 kilns. In April, 2012, when clearing up the north Grand Canal, people discovered 3 ancient sunken ships of the Ming Dynasty from the ancient channel in Zhangwan Village in Beichen District, Tianjin. After the further excavation by the archaeologists, nearly a thousand pieces of relics and specimens made in copper, iron, porcelain, pottery, bone, wood and bamboo from the Yuan, Ming and Qing dynasties were discovered. Judging according to the shipments and the size and shape of the ship, which was possible to be the barge used for inland grain shipping in the Ming Dynasty. These ancient sunken ships witness the development and vicissitude of the Grand Canal in thousand years' time, and provide valuable information for the study of the grain shipping and watercraft history.

## > 清代大运河的衰落

明朝灭亡后，清王朝也建都北京。清朝初期是大运河历史上漕运的全盛时期。清朝的漕运机构、管理制度、水源、路线工程设施、防

• 康熙帝像
Portrait of Emperor Kangxi

## > Decline of the Grand Canal in the Qing Dynasty

After the perishing of the Ming Dynasty, Beijing was also chosen as capital of the Qing Dynasty. The grain shipping was developed to its peak during the early Qing Dynasty. The shipping institution, management system, water sources, project route and flood protection of the grain shipping in the Qing Dynasty were almost same with the old system adopted by the Ming Dynasty. Like the middle and late Ming Dynasty, the grain shipping history of the Qing Dynasty was a story of fighting against the flood of the Yellow River. The Grand Canal of the Qing Dynasty could be divided into nine sections, which were the Datong Canal, Huitong Canal, Jiahe Canal, Xuhong Canal, Lvhong Canal, Huai'an Canal, Gaobao Canal, Guayi Canal, Danyang Canal and Zhejiang Canal, ranking from

《通惠河漕运图卷》【局部】沈喻（清）
*Drawing of Grain Shipping on Tonghui* [Partial] *Canal* by Shen Yu (Qing Dynasty, 1616-1911)

洪等方面完全依照明朝旧制，大同小异。清朝的漕运史与明朝中后期一样，也是一段与黄河水患相抗争的奋斗史。清朝的大运河分为九段管理，由北向南依次为大通河、会通河、泇河、徐洪、吕洪、淮安运河、高宝运河、瓜仪运河、丹阳运河和浙江运河。

康熙帝继位后，黄河仍旧时常发生水患，1665年到1676年间，黄

north to south.

After the Emperor Kangxi inherited the throne, the floods of the Yellow River were still frequent. As from 1665 to 1676, the Yellow River breached for six times, Kangxi dispatched Jin Fu to manage the river control project. Jin Fu massively cleaned the riverbed and excavated new canals, and finally enabled the grain to smoothly reach Beijing again. During the 52 years reign of Kangxi, he was deeply

● 山东台儿庄运河上的步云桥（图片提供：微图）
The Buyun Birdge on the Grand Canal of Taierzhuang, Shandong Province

河就曾六次决口。康熙帝任命靳辅主持治河工程，大力清理河道，开挖新渠，终于使漕粮又可以顺利到达北京。康熙帝在亲政的52年时间里，非常关心漕运，在巡察江南时也曾屡次亲临运河工地视察，因此大运河在康熙年间得到了良好的维护。为了保证漕运，运河大堤被不断增高。而且为了保证运河的水量，朝廷往往切断运河两岸农业用水，禁止运河水用于农田灌溉。这一举措引起了两岸百姓极大的不满。乾隆年间，为了缓解民怨，清政府设置了官闸与民闸，雨水丰沛时，运河水官民分用，到了冬春旱季运河水浅的时候，则暂时关闭民闸，以保证运河水位正常。

　　顺治、康熙、雍正、乾隆四位皇帝在位的150多年间，是清朝漕运最为繁忙的时期。为了维护这条大运河，清王朝特别设立了机构庞大的运河管理部门，以及为数众多的运河管理人员。投入维护大运河的费用更是多得惊人。每年押运漕粮的漕卒要几十万人，用于维护运河的民工和守卫大堤的士兵也有几十万人。有时重载的大船经过深浅

attentive to the grain shipping, and had performed several times of field visit to the River South Region in person. As a result, the Grand Canal was well maintained within the Kangxi Period. To guarantee to grain shipping, the canal levee was constructed higher and higher; and the court usually prohibited the irrigation by cutting down the agricultural water supply to assure the water volume of the canal, prompting criticism from the people living by the canal. During the Qianlong Period, in order to ease the social grievance, the canal was set up with official sluice and civilian sluice. When there was plentiful rain, the canal water could be used by both the official and citizen; in dry season, the civilian sluice would be shortly shut down to guarantee the water level of the canal.

During the 150 years reign of the four emperors Shunzhi, Kangxi, Yongzheng and Qianlong, the grain shipping of the Qing Dynasty was most hectic. To maintain this Grand Canal, the government of the Qing Dynasty specially established the huge canal management department, recruited numerous personnel to manage the canal, and invested striking financial resources. There were hundreds of thousands of

不平的河道或逆水行船的时候，往往需要三四百名纤夫来拉着漕船前进。因此清政府每年为漕运投入的人力不下百万，为此投入的钱粮更是数以亿计。虽然花费巨大，但是大运河为沿岸城镇的经济发展带来的好处却更大。

当时运河沿岸各城镇的码头上都停泊着大、中、小各种型号的船只，岸上也是车水马龙，四方宾客云集。码头附近的客栈、酒楼档次是最高的，码头附近市场上的商品也是最齐全的，各种娱乐场所也聚集在码头周围。不仅商人使用运河，赶考的学生、游山玩水的文士、达官贵人、外国使节，以至于皇亲国戚、当朝天子、嫔妃都通过大运河出行。大运河成为当时一条最快捷便利的集游玩、旅行、运输为一体的水上交通线。

清乾隆末期开始，黄河的水患越来越严重，到了道光年间，运河河床已经被泥沙淤积得很高了，随时可能决口。朝廷不得已开启海上航线运输漕粮。到19世纪中叶，大运河已经处于半瘫痪状态，当时欧洲殖民国家已用坚船利炮打开了中

soldiers escorting the grain shipping every year, and same numbers of civilian workers and soldiers were needed to maintain the canal and guide the levee. Sometimes when the large heavy load ship was passing the section with uneven depth or sailing against the current, three of four hundred trackers should be needed to drag the ship forward. Although the grain shipping required over a million labors and hundreds of millions of wealth per year, the Grand Canal created greater benefit for the economic development of the towns by the canal.

The wharfs in the towns by the canal of that time berthed the ships in different sizes and various models, and the banks were crowed with people and vehicles from all over the country. The restaurants near the wharfs were first rank-highest quality, and the markets by the wharfs possessed the most complete goods. Various entertainment venues were all gathered surrounding the wharfs. Besides the merchants, the Grand Canal was also used by the students, scholars, high officials and noble lords and diplomatic envoys, and even the members of the imperial house, the emperors and the imperial concubines all traveled by the Grand Canal, which made it the most

国的大门。比起内河漕运，利用国外的海轮运输漕粮确实便利得多。另一方面，清政府忙于清剿各地的农民起义，军费浩大，无力再治理

convenient water traffic line of that time, concentrating the touring, travelling and transportation functions in one body.

From the late Qianlong Period in the Qing Dynasty, the flood disaster of the Yellow River became more and more serious. During the Daoguang Period, the riverbed of the canal had been piled up by the sediment and was in danger of breaching at any time, and the court had no choice but to turn to ocean shipping. By the middle of 19th century, the Grand Canal had been half paralyzed. Meanwhile the European colonial powers of that time had also burst into China with sophisticated weapons. Because the foreign ocean steamers were more convenient than the inland canal, and as

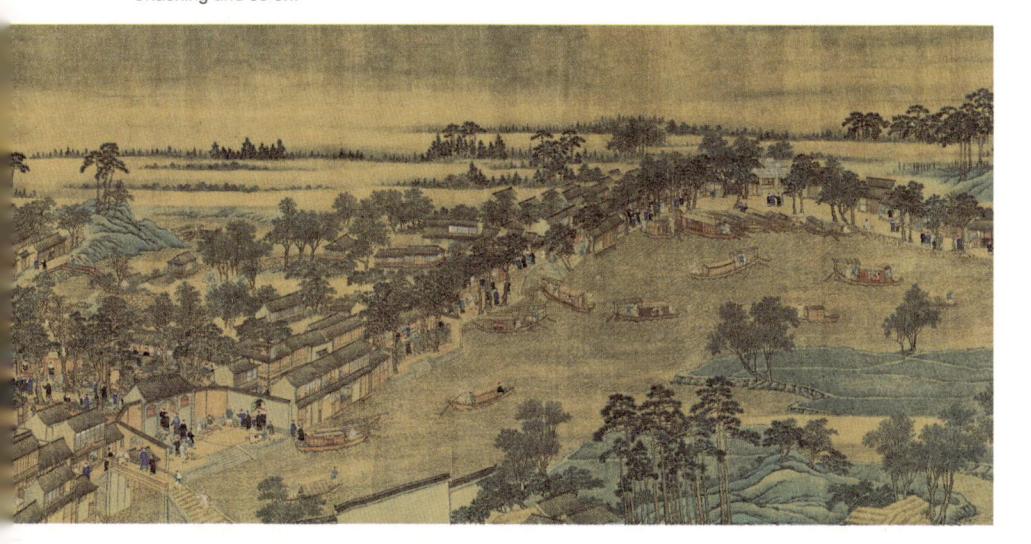

- 《康熙南巡图卷》【局部】（清）

  康熙帝在1684年到1707年的20多年间，曾先后六次南巡，其主要目的是加强清政府对运河以及江南地区的统治。其出巡线路基本上是沿着京杭大运河线路行进，途经济南、淮阴、扬州、苏州、杭州、绍兴等地。

  *Painting of Emperor Kangxi's Southern Inspection Tour* [Partial] (Qing Dynasty, 1616-1911)

  The Emperor Kangxi used to inspect the South China for six times during the over 20 years from 1684 to 1707, aiming to enhance the domination of the Qing Dynasty in the River South Region. The route of Kangxi was basically flowing the Beijing-Hangzhou Grand Canal, passing through Jinan, Huaiyin, Yangzhou, Suzhou, Hangzhou, Shaoxing and so on.

黄河与修补运河，内河漕运由此中断。光绪三十四年（1908年），清政府决定漕粮的运输全走海路，大运河的漕运机构以及各地维护官员全部撤销，大运河的漕运使命就此画上了句号。

the government of the Qing Dynasty was busy suppressing the peasant uprisings all over the country, having no time and money to control the flood and maintain the canal, the grain shipping by inland canal was terminated since then. In 1908, as the whole grain shipping was proceeding by sea and the canal institutions and maintenance personnel were abolished, the mission of the Grand Canal no longer existed.

## > 大运河的新生

清朝末年，京汉、津浦等铁路修建以后，清朝政府不再关心大运河的命运，任其荒废。运河河道越来越窄，最窄处不足10米，运输能力大减，不少河段不能通航。山东境内的部分河段已淤成平地，即使水量较大、通航条件较好的江苏省内河段也只能通行小木帆船。

中华人民共和国成立后，政府制定了改造大运河的计划，对运河很多区段进行了疏浚、扩展，而且沿河建设了不少航闸和现代化码头。1988年底，京杭运河和钱塘江沟通工程顺利完成，构成了以杭州为中心、以京杭运河与长江、黄河、淮河、海河、钱塘江五大水系相连通的水运网。在煤炭、建材、盐、日用工业品、粮油和其他农副

## > Rebirth of the Grand Canal

In the late Qing Dynasty, after the Jing-Han and Tianjin-Pukou railways were completed, the government of the Qing Dynasty no longer cared the destiny to the canal and watched it lying waste. The channel of the Grand Canal became narrower day by day, and the narrowest section had been only 10 meters wide. The transportation capacity of the canal was hugely weakened, many sections couldn't bear ships for sailing, and the partial section within the Shandong Province had been silted up into flat ground. Even the section in Jiangsu Province with the best navigation condition enabled only small wooden boats to pass.

After the birth of the People's Republic of China, the government formulated a plan to reform the Grand Canal, dredged and expanded many

• 水运繁忙的大运河（图片提供：微图）
Busy Grand Canal

sections of the canal, and constructed quite a few of sluices and modern wharfs for the canal. At the end of 1988, the project connecting the Grand Canal and Qiantang River was completed, forming the water transport network concatenating the Grand Canal and the five major water systems of the Yangtze River, Yellow River, Huaihe River, Haihe River and Qiantang River. The Grand Canal still played an essential role in the short-distance transporting of coals, building materials, salt, manufactured goods for daily use, grain and oil and other subsidiary agricultural products. By now, except for the two sections from Beijing to Tianjin and Linqing to the Yellow River, the rest sections of the Grand Canal have all been dredged. After the implementing of the South-North Water Diversion Project, which is still in programming, in the future, the Grand Canal will turn into the major water transferring line and glow the vitality of youth once again.

产品的中短途运输方面，大运河还发挥着不可取代的作用。现在，整个大运河，除北京到天津、临清到黄河两段外，其余河段均已通航。正在建设中的中国南水北调东线工程实施后，大运河将成为重要的输水线路，重新焕发出青春的活力。

# 大运河与中国名城
# The Grand Canal and Its Major Cities

　　大运河是世界上开凿最早、规模最大、流程最长的人工河流，它见证了中华两千多年的历史风云，孕育了沿河两岸一座座璀璨明珠般的名城。从北到南，沿着大运河，人们可以领略到运河两岸名城的独特风貌。

The Grand Canal possesses the earliest excavation time, largest scale and longest flow distance among the man-made rivers in the world. It has witnessed over 2000 years of history of China, and bred the numerous prosperous ancient cities aside its channel. Travelling through the Grand Canal from north to south, one will appreciate the unique styles and features of the major cities by the canal.

## > 北京

中国的首都北京是大运河的起点，而北京城区西北部的什刹海则是元代漕粮运输的终点码头。什刹海由前海、后海、积水潭组成，其中积水潭在元代时是一个热闹非凡的水港。元世祖忽必烈定都大都

## > Beijing

Beijing, the capital of China, is the origin of the Grand Canal, and the Shichahai Lake in the northwest downtown of Beijing was the terminal wharf of the grain shipping transportation in the Yuan Dynasty. The Shichahai Lake is constituted by the Qianhai Lake, Houhai Lake and Jishui Pool, among which the Jishui Pool was a water port of prosperity during the Yuan Dynasty. After choosing Dadu (today's Beijing) as capital, the Kublai Khan dispatched the hydrauic expert Guo Shoujing to manage the excavation of the Tonghui Canal, in order to transport the grain in the River South Region to the capital. The ships from the

• 风景优美的什刹海
Beautiful Shichahai Lake

- **积水潭万宁桥**

万宁桥俗称"后门桥",是积水潭的入口,设有闸口,漕船要进入积水潭必须从桥下经过。当时的积水潭水深面阔,南来北往的粮船、商船云集。

**Wanning Bridge on Jishui Pool**

The Wanning Bridge is also called "Back-door Bridge", is the entrance of the Jishui Pool and set up with water-gate. It's only route for the grain-ships entering the Jishui Pool. The Jishui Pool in ancient time had wide and deep water and was crowded with grain and merchant ships from everywhere.

(今北京)后,为了将江南的粮食运进京城,水利专家郭守敬奉命主持开凿了通惠河,由南方沿大运河北上的漕运船只经通惠河可直接驶入大都城内的积水潭。明代,明成祖迁都北京后,下令不准漕船入城,而将大通桥附近的护城河沿岸变为漕船停泊的码

south could directly enter into the Jishui Poor within the downtown of Dadu by the Tonghui Canal. In the Ming Dynasty, after switching the capital to Beijing, the Emperor Chengzu of Ming prohibited ships from entering into the city, and transformed the city moat bank near the Datong Bridge to the wharf for grain ships. As a result, the Jishui Pool had

• 南新仓
Nanxincang Granary

头，积水潭逐渐被废弃，成为水源不通的内湖。

大批粮食通过运河运至北京后，便会存入京师各处粮仓。其中，南新仓就是大运河"南粮北运"的终点站。南新仓俗称"东门仓"，位于北京东四十条，于明永乐七年（1409年）在元代北太仓的基础上起建，至今已有600多年历史。那里现存古粮仓9座，是北京现

gradually been abandoned and became an internal lake with no water source.

After being shipped to Beijing by canal, the vast grain would be stored in various granaries. Among which, the Nanxin Granary was the terminal of the "South-North Grain Transportation". The Nanxin Granary, commonly called the "East Gate Granary", locates in East Fortieth Lane in Beijing, and was built in 1409 in the Ming Dynasty over 600 years

存规模最大、保存最好的皇家粮仓，也是京都史、漕运史、仓储史的历史见证。

北京东部的通州是北运河的起点，漕运的繁荣极大地促进了古通州的繁盛。自古漕运乃国脉所系，元朝以来，南方各省漕船直抵通州，通州运河呈现出千舟万楫云集的盛况，因而通州城的商业十分发达。清代康熙皇帝曾巡幸通州20余次。乾隆时期通州知府尹澍就曾在

ago on the basis of the Beitai Granary of the Yuan Dynasty. 9 ancient granaries are still preserved in this place, which are the largest and best maintained royal granaries in Beijing, and the testimony of Beijing, grain shipping and warehousing histories.

The Tongzhou District in eastern Beijing is the starting point of the north canal, and the prosperity of the grain shipping extremely boosted the development of the ancient Tongzhou. Since ancient times, the grain shipping on the old canal had always been the lifeblood of China. Starting from the Yuan Dynasty, grain-ships from the southern provinces had been able to directly reach Tongzhou, and the countless ships on the Tongzhou Canal

- **通州运河边的燃灯佛舍利塔**（摄影：陈闻达）
燃灯佛舍利塔坐落于通州北城运河的西岸，因塔身正南券洞内供奉燃灯佛而得名。此塔始建于北周时期，距今已有1400多年的历史，目前已经成为通州古城的象征。

**Dipamkara Pagoda by Tongzhou Canal**
The Dipamkara Pagoda locates on the west canal bank to the north of Tongzhou and get its name for the Dipamkara consecrating within the hole on the south tower body. This tower was built in the Northern Zhou Dynasty over 1400 years ago, and has become the symbol of the ancient Tongzhou town.

诗中描述通州运河"漕艇贾舶如云集，万国梯航满潞川"。在通州运河上，漕船携带的南方土特产数量众多，通州城内外形成了许多货栈和市场。如明代嘉靖年间，通州城

displayed the scenes of prosperity. The Emperor Kangxi of Qing had inspected Tongzhou in person for over 20 times. For this reason, the business industry in Tongzhou was also well developed. Yin

- **通州运河八里桥**

八里桥又称"永通桥"，是一座三孔的券形石拱桥，建于明正统十一年（1446年）。此桥中间的桥洞高达8.5米，而左右两孔仅高3.5米，相差悬殊，这是专为漕运的需要设计的。因为通惠河上的运粮船多为帆船，工匠将桥的中孔建造得相当高，漕船可直出直入，有所谓"八里桥不落桅"之说。

**Bali Bridge on Tongzhou Canal**

The Bali Bridge (also called "Yongtong Bridge") is a three-hole stone arch bridge and was built in 1446. The middle hole of the bridge is 8.5 meters high, but the holes on both sides are only 3.5 meters high; the drop is huge. Such design was for the need of grain shipping. As the grain-ships on the Tonghui Canal were mostly sailing boats, the craftsmen built the middle hole high enough to enable the grain-ships to pass without furling the sails.

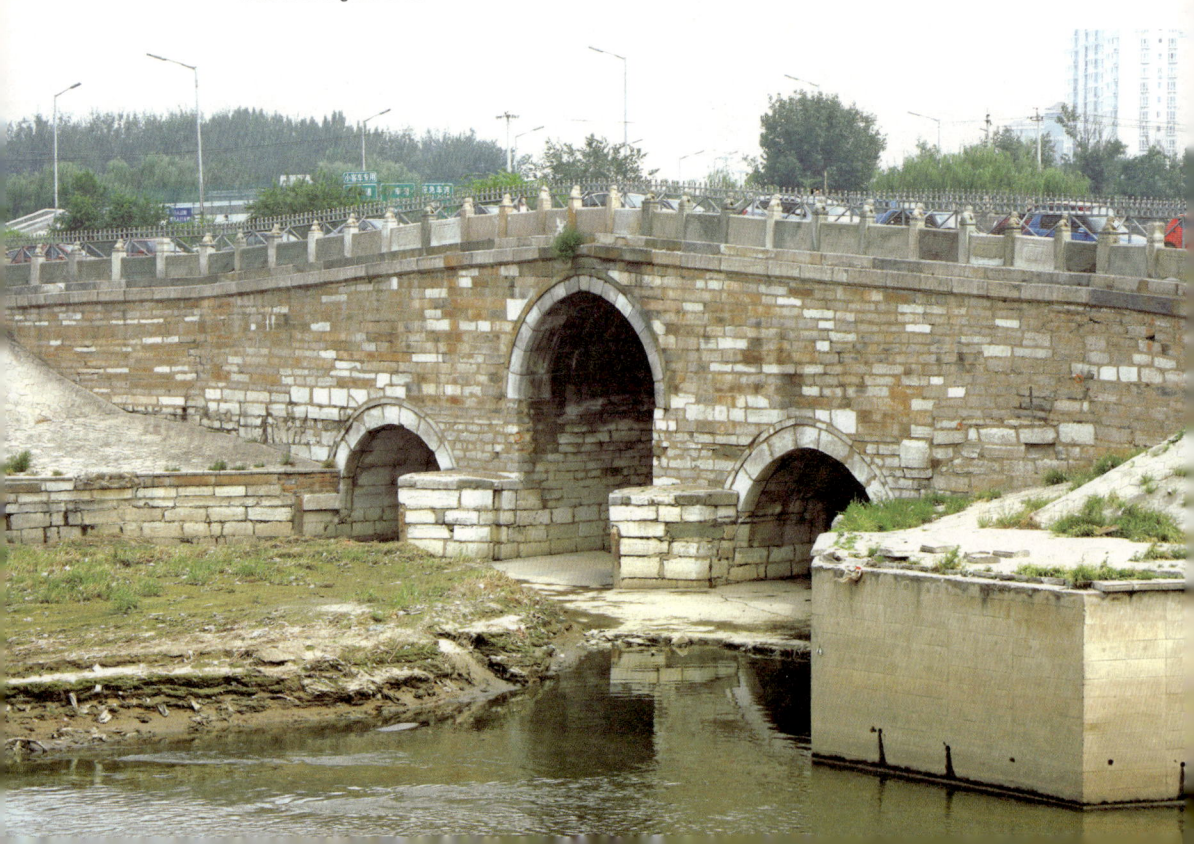

八里桥上的镇兽
Stone Carved Beats on Bali Bridge

东垣外的运河西岸形成的粮食市，是北京城区和郊县最大的民间私营粮食货栈。

　　古运河还赋予了通州重要的政治、军事地位。通州东濒北运河，西距京城咫尺之遥，是通往京城的重要门径，保卫京师的军事要塞。来往北京的官员、赴京应试的举子，甚至外国来华使臣，大多乘舟至通州，然后在通州弃舟乘轿进京。

Shu, the magistrate of Tongzhou during Qianlong Period, used to describe the Tongzhou Canal in his poem as "grain and merchant ships come together in crowds, covering all the waters". The grain-ships brought in incalculable local special products, forming masses of markets and warehouses within and out of the Tongzhou town. For example, during the Jiajing Period of the Ming Dynasty, a grain market was set up by the west canal bank east to Tongzhou, which has been the largest civil private grain warehouse in the downtown and suburbs of Beijing.

　　The ancient canal also provided Tongzhou with significant political and military positions. Closing to the canal in the east and the capital in the west, Tongzhou is an important pathway to and the military fortress to protect Beijing. Most officials, students, and even the foreign envoys heading to Beijing should come through the canal and transfer onto sedan chairs in Tongzhou.

## > 天津

　　天津位于北京之南，处于海河各支流的交汇处。远古时期，天津地区还是一片大海。约在4000多年前，现在的天津市区所在地逐渐露出海底成为陆地。而最迟到战国时期，这里已有先民劳作生息。西汉时期，天津的地域隶属渔阳郡。金代海陵王建都中都（即北京），在海河边设立直沽寨，成为京畿南部的军事重镇。

　　为了解决粮食供应问题，金人修建了由永济渠到达今天津三岔河口的北运河。通过这条运河，南方的粮食便可运往中都。明建文二年（1400年），燕王朱棣在此渡过大运河南下争夺皇位，揭开了"靖难之役"的序幕。三年后，朱棣攻下南京，即位为帝，为纪念起兵之

## > Tianjin

Tianjin locates south to Beijing, and lies in the junction area of the tributaries of the Haihe River. In remote antiquity, Tianjin was still a piece of the sea. About 4000 years ago, the place of today's Tianjin City gradually rose above the sea. By the Warring States Period, there were people residing here. In the Western Han Dynasty, the region of Tianjin was under the jurisdiction of Yuyang Prefecture. After establishing Zhongdu (today's Beijing), the King of Hailing from the Jin Dynasty set up Zhigu Village by the sea, which became the important military town guarding the south of the capital.

　　To the resolving of the grain issue, the Jin Dynasty constructed the North Canal from the Yongji Canal to the Sancha River Mouth in today's Tianjin. Through this canal, the grain in the south could be shipped directly to Zhongdu.

● 天津城里的老街区
Old Street in Downtown of Tianjin

地，于永乐二年（1404）将此地赐名为"天津"，即"天子经过的渡口"之意。在三岔河口西南的小直沽一带，天津开始筑城设卫，称"天津卫"。

京杭大运河的北运河和南运河在天津汇聚，又在这里被海河送入

In 1400, the Emperor Zhu Di departed the south from this place fight for the throne, started the "Jingnan Campaign". Three years later, Zhu Di conquered Nanjing and accessed to the throne. To commemorate the starting place of the revolt, in 1404, Zhu Di renamed the place "Tianjin", which means "the ferry-place of the emperor" in Chinese. After that, a city was constructed in Xiaozhigu region southwest to the Sancha River Mouth and was named "Tianjin Wei".

The northern and southern sections of the Grand Canal meet in Tianjin, and are brought into the Bohai Sea together by the Haihe River. For this reason, the Haihe River had become the only route connecting the canal shipping and ocean shipping. The junction place of the southern Grand Canal, Haihe River and northern Grand Canal is called the Sancha River Mouth, where was the only route for the grain-ships going to the capital in ancient times and used to be extremely busy day and night. According to historical records, when grain shipping was still booming, the North Canal from Tianjin to Tongzhou was bearing 20 thousand grain-ships, 10 thousand merchant ships and 120 thousand soldiers per year. The rise of Tianjin cannot be

085

大运河与中国名城
The Grand Canal and Its Major Cities

渤海。因此海河成为连接运河航运与海运的唯一通道。南运河、海河、北运河的交汇口称为"三岔河口",是古代漕运进京船只的必经之地。当年的三岔河口帆樯林立,船只往来昼夜不停,一片繁忙景象。据记载,漕运发达时期,从天津到通州的北运河每年要承载2万艘运粮的漕船,官兵12万人次,连同商船共3万艘。天津城的兴起与漕运有着密切的关系,可以说,天津是运河载来的城市。

天津的城市布局是伴随着运河与漕运而逐渐形成的。海河与运河沿岸附近的聚落密度和规模都较大,如南运河沿岸的静海、独流等都是明代漕运的码头,人口密集,经济发达。而北运河沿岸的"老米店"为元代漕运屯米处,"崇粮务"是糟粮交易场,"木厂"是漕运存放木材的地方,"南口哨"是保护漕运的哨所……

三岔河口西岸坐落着著名的天后宫。这是一座供奉海上女神妈祖的道教宫观,始建于元后期,明清时几经重修。它与福建湄洲屿的妈祖庙、台湾北港镇的朝天宫,合称

separated with the grain shipping. In a manner of speaking, Tianjin was bred up by the canal.

The urban layout of Tianjin was gradually formed complying with the canal and grain shipping. The area near the banks of the Haihe River and the canal is greater in urban density and scales. For example, the places of Jinghai, Duliu and so on by the south canal were wharfs during the Ming Dynasty, and had dense population and advanced economy. Besides, by the north canal, the *Laomidian* was a grain warehouse in the Yuan Dynasty. The *Tiaoliangwu* was used to be a grain market, the *Muchang* was used to be a wood storage, and the *Nanshaokou* was a sentry protecting the grain shipping.

By the west bank of the Sancha River Mouth there lies a famous Tianhou Temple, which is a Taoist temple consecrating the sea goddess Matsu. The temple was firstly built in the late Yuan Dynasty, and reconstructed for several times during the Ming and Qing dynasties. The Tianhou Temple, the Matsu Temple in Meizhou Island in Fujian Province and the Chaotian Temple in Beigang Town in Taiwan Province, are jointly called the three

为中国三大妈祖庙。妈祖是古代传说中的护海女神，古时每逢漕船平安抵达三岔河口，水手们就要在宫前广场酬神赛会，南北各地商品也云集于此，热闹非凡。明、清以来，天后宫一带一直是天津市最繁华的街区，也是天津城市发展的见证。

有桥有水，便会有渡口。天津早年的渡口分为私渡、官渡和义渡三种。私渡是最早出现的，在自然村落形成时便出现了。官渡是官家

major Matsu temples of China. Matsu is the sea goddess from the ancient legend. In ancient times when the grain-ships safely arrived at the Sancha River Mouth, the sailors would hold ceremonies in the front of the temple. Meanwhile the products from the north and south were also gathered here, made the place extreme hilarious. Since the Ming and Qing dynasties, the Tianhou Temple area has always been the most prosperous urban district of Tianjin and the witness of city development.

- 天津天后宫（图片提供：微图）
  Tianjin Tianhou Temple

● 天津三岔河口（图片提供：微图）
The Sancha River Mouth in Tianjin

为方便驿使往来设立的，而义渡则是由僧人募捐或地方绅士捐资修建的。在这些渡口中，北马头渡的地位尤其重要。江南来的漕船要经过此处的南运河，后经三岔河口转北运河抵达京师。来往的行人、客商多在此地停留歇息、买卖交易，形成"钞关桥上人如鹜，商船打鼓马头住"的胜景。天津为此专门开设了十大集市，也留下了"天津卫天天赶大集"的民谚。

Wherever there are water and bridges, there is ferry-place. The early ferries of Tianjin were divided into three varieties, the private ferry, official ferry and charitable ferry. The private ferries were the earliest, emerging together with the arising of the natural villages. The official ferries were set up by the government for the convenience of the mounted couriers. The construction of the charitable ferries were donated by the monks or local gentlemen. Among these

在天津运河沿岸，设有多处粮仓，如南仓、北仓、上仓等。北仓在北辰区北运河东岸，坐东朝西，建有仓房48座，共计240间，储粮40万石，是天津最大的传输、储存、备赈粮仓。古代一到灾年，这里便会设粥厂赈灾济民，最多的时候，一天能有上万灾民来这里领粥。南仓的位置与北仓相近，从元明两代起，那里就成为漕运码头和储粮之地。

运河天津段沿岸最为著名的文化遗产，就是闻名世界的"杨柳青

- **天津十八街麻花**

天津的美食也很有名，比如狗不理包子、十八街麻花、崩豆、小宝栗子都是不容错过的美味。

**Tianjin 18th Street Fried Dough Twist**

Tianjin is also famous for its cuisine. For example, the Goubuli's stuffed buns, 18th Street Fried Dough Twists, beans and Xiaobao Chestnuts all shouldn't be missed.

ferries, the Beimatou Ferry was the most important one. The grain-ships from the River South Region should transfer from the south canal to the north canal at the Sancha River Mouth. The passing people and merchants usually rest in this place and bargained transactions, forming the famous scenery of "crowded people on Chaoguan Bridge and ships resting in Beimatou". The Tianjin government also specially set up 10 major markets here, which left the proverb of "everyday in Tianjin is market day".

By the Tianjin section of the canal, they were set up with many granaries, like the South Granary, North Granary, Shang Granary and so on. The North Granary locates on the east bank of the North Canal in Beichen District, sitting toward the west, which was equipped with 48 warehouses, 240 rooms. The North Granary could store forty thousand *Dan* of grain, and was the largest transportation, storage and emergency relief granary of Tianjin. In ancient times, when a disaster struck, the North Granary would set up porridge factories to relieve the victims. Over ten thousand victims could be attracted here in a single day at most. The South Granary locates near the North Granary, and had been the grain

年画"。杨柳青年画诞生于天津市西20千米的杨柳青镇,始于元末明初,距今已有600多年的历史。据说当时有民间艺人避难来到杨柳青镇,逢年过节就刻印门神、灶王年画出售,镇上的人争相模仿。到了明永乐年间,大运河重新疏通,南方精致的纸张和颜料运到此地,使杨柳青的年画艺术得到发展。到了清代中期全盛时期,全镇连同附近的32个村子,"家家会点染,户户善丹青",画店鳞次栉比。杨柳青年画将传统的套印制年画改为仅印画面的轮廓,并将着色部分都改成

• 杨柳青年画《果仙敬月》
Yangliuqing New Year Picture *Immortals Consecrating the Moon*

shipping wharf and grain storage since the Yuan and Ming dynasties.

The most important cultural heritage in the Tianjin section areas of the canal is the world famous "New Year Pictures in Yangliuqing", which was established over 600 years ago, between the late Yuan Dynasty and the early Ming Dynasty, in Yangliuqing Town 20 kilometers west to the downtown of Tianjin. According to the legend, the folk artists of that time came to Yangliuqing Town seeking asylum. Every holiday, these artists sold the New Year pictures painted with immortals, which were widely imitated among the town. During the Yongle Period of the Ming Dynasty, the re-dredging of the Grand Canal brought the fine paper and pigment to this place, boosted the New Year picture art of Yangliuqing. By the middle Qing Dynasty, this kind of art reached its peak. The whole town and the 32 villages surrounding it were crowded with painting shops, and every family were good at painting. Different with the traditional batching products, the Yangliuqing New Year pictures were only printed the outlines of the frames, and adopted handwork painting in the

手工彩绘，令整体色彩变得鲜艳、饱满、富有生机。

运河不仅是连接南北经济的运输生命线，同时也养育了沿岸的百姓。天津地区的沿河人家除了利用运河灌溉、水运、打渔外，沿河湿地盛产的芦苇也成为人们谋生的重要物资，苇席和苇叶编织的各种物品一直是天津著名的土特产。驰名全国的天津大白菜、天津冬菜、独流老醋、沙窝萝卜等都与运河水有着密切的关系。

coloring process, which made the integral color vivid, plump and lively.

The canal was not only the transport lifeline connecting the north-south economy, but also bred the people by the bank. The people in Tianjin region took use of the canal for irrigation, water transportation and fishing. Meanwhile, the reed by the canal also became an important material for the locals to make a living. Various kinds of handmade crafts weaved by weed have always been the famous local specialties of Tianjin. The nationwide famous Tianjin specialties such as Tianjin cabbage, Tianjin preserved vegetable, Duliu old vinegar, Shawo radish and so on all have a close relationship with the canal.

## > 沧州

大运河出了天津，就进入河北沧州。大运河在河北境内的河段长435千米，其中沧州段就有253千米，是大运河流经里程最长的城市。沧州段运河又称"南运河"，从南到北贯穿沧州。这里的运河最早开凿于三国时期，隋代在此基础上进行疏浚，时称"永济渠"，宋元时改称"御河"，明朝改称"卫河"，到了清朝则称"运河"。

沧州有着丰富的运河文化遗存，至今保留着完整的古代河道、水利工程设施以及多达百余处的文化古迹。在沧州运河岸边，有大小渡口十余个，如莲池渡、菜市口渡、枣寺庙渡、白家口渡、戴家园渡等都是有名的渡口。随着运河的改造，如今这些渡口已经不复存在

## > Cangzhou

Deviating from Tianjin, the Grand Canal enters into Cangzhou in Hebei Province. The canal of Hebei section is 435 kilometers long. Among which the Cangzhou section is 253 kilometers, which is the longest range of all the cities by the canal. The canal of Cangzhou section is also called the South Canal, cutting through the city from south to north. This section was firstly excavated in the Three Kingdoms Period, then dredged by the Sui Dynasty and called Yongji Canal. After that, it was renamed Yuhe in the Song Dynasty, Weihe in the Ming Dynasty, and Yunhe in the Qing Dynasty.

There are vast canal cultural relics in Cangzhou. The complete ancient canal, water conservancy facilities and over a hundred cultural relics are preserved till now. More than ten ferries in different

了，取而代之的是一座座飞架东西的大桥。在如今的运河上出现了花园大桥、新华桥、永济桥、彩虹桥、解放桥等桥梁，桥上车来人往，川流不息。

沧州是全国闻名的"武术之乡"。沧州自古就是兵家必争之地，当地百姓为自救自保，往往从

sizes could be found by the bank of the canal in Cangzhou, the Lotus Ferry, Caishikou Ferry, Zaosi Temple Ferry, Baijiakou Ferry and Daijiayuan Ferry for example were all famous. Along with the reform of the canal, these ferries gradually disappeared and had been replaced by the modern bridges. The newly emerged Garden Bridge, Xinhua

- 沧州铁狮子（图片提供：微图）

铁狮子位于沧州旧州城内，通高5.48米，总重量达29.3吨，铸造于五代后周广顺三年（953年），距今已有1000多年的历史。现在这尊铁狮子已经成为沧州城的标志。

**Iron Lion in Cangzhou**

The Iron Lion locates in the old town of Cangzhou, is 5.48 meters high and 29.3 tons weight. It was cast in 953 in the Five dynasties over 1000 years ago, and has become the symbol of Cangzhou till now.

小练习攻防格斗等技能，所以沧州习武之风十分兴盛。大运河纵穿沧州，沧州也成为周边省份商品流通的必经之地和集散中心，因此沧州保镖、装运等行业兴盛，从而促进了沧州武术的发展。

Bridge, Yongji Bridge, Rainbow Bridge and Liberation Bridge for example crossing the canal are very busy now.

The national famous "Home of Kong Fu" Cangzhou has always been a town of great military importance since ancient times. The local people commonly learnt martial arts from childhood. As a result, the atmosphere of martial art in Cangzhou is very prosperous. As the Grand Canal cutting through Cangzhou made it a must place to pass or distributing center of the circulating commodities from the surrounding provinces, the bodyguard and escorting business were well developed, which also boosted the martial arts development in Cangzhou.

## > 德州

德州位于黄河下游，山东省西北部，是山东的北大门。德州城历史悠久，在原始社会，德州地区就是新石器文化遗址龙山文化的发祥地之一。秦汉以来，德州一直为历代州府治所。

- 龙山文化红陶鬶（新石器时代）
Red Pottery *Gui* (cooker) from Longshan Culture (Neolithic Age)

## > Dezhou

Dezhou, located in the lower reaches of the Yellow River in northwest Shandong Province, is the north entrance of Shandong and has a long history. In the primitive society, the Dezhou Region was one of the birth places of the Neolithic cultural site Longshan Culture. Since the Qin and Han dynasties, Dezhou had always been the state seat in various dynasties.

The Dezhou ancient canal was firstly built in the Sui and Tang dynasties, and became prosperous in the Ming and Qing dynasties. The rolling water crossing Dezhou made it the first gateway of the canal heading south from Beijing. In 1129, the court of the Jin Dynasty set up the Jiangling Granary on today's Beichang Street in Dezhou to reserve the grain from Shandong and Henan provinces. After the completion of the

● 德州"神京门户"牌坊（图片提供：全景正片）
"Portal of Capital" Memorial Archway in Dezhou

德州古运河开凿于隋唐，繁荣于明清，滚滚河水从德州市区穿过，德州成为顺京城水路南下的首道关口。1129年，金在德州市今天北厂街设将陵仓，储存山东、河南两省的漕粮。会通河开凿后，陵州仓储粮规模进一步扩大，成为元代重要的漕粮中转站。明代时，德州粮仓是大运河上的四大粮仓之一，

Huitong Canal, the scale of this granary was further expanded, making it an important grain transferring station of the Yuan Dynasty. In the Ming Dynasty, the granary of Dezhou was one of the four major granaries by the canal, could store and transfer over a million *Dan* of grain and possessed the function to regulate the supply of the capital. Vast of grain-ships, privately owned ships and merchant

存储和转运的粮食达几十万至数百万石，起着调节粮食余缺、满足京城供应的作用。大量漕船、民船和商船在德州停留交易，使德州百业兴旺，德州的经济伴随着漕运的兴盛而繁荣。

老德州有三座运河桥，一是建于明洪武年间的广川浮桥，二是建于清雍正年间的九达天衢桥，三是建于近代的广安桥。如今，这三座桥都已退出历史舞台，只剩下那些历经沧桑的青石，似乎在诉说着运河古今的变化。

ships stayed in Dezhou for transactions, boosting the economy and industries in Dezhou.

There were three canal bridges in ancient Dezhou. One was the Guangchuan Floating Bridge built in the Ming Dynasty, another one was the Jiuda-Tianqu Bridge built in the Yongzheng Period of the Qing Dynasty, and the third one was the Guang'an Bridge built in recent period. Till now, these three bridges had all withdrawn from the historical stage, left the dilapidated stones showing the history of time.

### 德州的苏禄王墓

古苏禄王国是位于今菲律宾苏禄群岛上的伊斯兰教国家。明成祖永乐十五年（1417年），苏禄群岛上的三位国王——东王巴都葛叭哈喇、西王麻哈喇葛麻丁、峒王巴都葛叭喇卜率家眷一行340多人组成友好使团，来到中国进行友好访问。他们来到北京，受到明成祖的隆重接待。在北京逗留了22天后，苏禄王一行乘船沿京杭大运河南下回国，东王在取道山东归国途中，不幸染病，病故于德州。明成祖闻讯深为哀悼，下令以藩王之礼厚葬东王。墓址位于今德州城北郊的长庄乡北营村。其后，东王长子率众回国，王妃及次子、三子留居德州守墓。清雍正九年（1731年），东王的后裔获得朝廷准许入籍中国，成为中华民族的一员，迄今已传至第21代。

## Tomb of King of Sulu State in Dezhou

The ancient Sulu State was an Islamic state locating on today's Sulu Archipelago in Philippines. In 1417, three kings from the Sulu Archipelago, the East King Badugebahala, West King Mahalagemading and Tong King Badugebalabu led the friendly mission of over 340 people to visit China, and were well treated by the Emperor Chengzu of Ming in Beijing. After staying in Beijing for 22 days, the Sulu kings left for south by ship through the Beijing-Hangzhou Grand Canal to return the country. When arriving at Shandong Province, the East King was infected with a disease and died in Dezhou. The Emperor Chengzu of Ming was sad when hearing his death, and gave orders to hold an elaborate funeral with the standards of the seigniors for him. The tomb was excavated in today's Beiying Village in Changzhuang County in the northern suburbs of Dezhou. After that, the eldest son of the East King returned his country, leaving the princess consort, the second and third sons in Dezhou guard the grave. In 1731 in the Qing Dynasty, the descendants of the East King were allowed by the court to join the Chinese nationality. Till now, they have already developed to the 21st generation.

• 山东德州苏禄王墓（图片提供：全景正片）
Tomb of King of Sulu State in Dezhou, Shandong Province

## > 临清

　　临清位于山东省西部，西汉初年即设县置，后赵建平元年（330年）因临近清河而改称"临清"。元代会通河与通惠河开凿完成后，处于会通河与卫河交汇处的临清一下成为水路要冲。明清时期，临清凭借大运河漕运兴盛而迅速崛起，成为运河沿岸最大的码头和商埠之

## > Linqing

Linqing lies in the west of Shandong Province. It became a county in the early Western Han Dynasty, and was renamed "Linqing" in 330, as it was close to the Qing River. After the completion of the Huitong Canal and Tonghui Canal in the Yuan Dynasty, Linqing located in the junction area of the Huitong Canal and Weihe River suddenly became the

- 18世纪末英国画师笔下的临清运河景象
  The Scenery of Canal in Linqing by English Painter During the End of 18th Century

北京故宫太和门广场
Supreme Harmony Gate Square in the Forbidden City, Beijing

一，南北货物汇集，经济发达，文化活动繁盛，人口最盛时达到数百万。成书于明代万历年间的古典小说《金瓶梅》，其故事的主要发生地就在临清。小说中写到临清的地方有很多，如第九十二回云："这临清市上，是个热闹繁华大码头去处，商贾往来、船只聚会之所，车辆辐辏之地，有三十二条花柳巷，七十二座管弦楼。"

临清不仅是当时重要的商贸流通中心，而且是最大的贡砖烧

waterway communications hub. During the Ming and Qing dynasties, for the prosperity of the grain shipping, Linqing rapidly rose to one of the largest wharfs and commercial ports by the canal with developed economy, flourishing culture and millions of population at its highest. The story of the classical fiction *The Golden Lotus* of the Ming Dynasty was based in Linqing and described the town in detail. For example, the chapter 92 mentioned that "a busy wharf lies in Linqing, crowded with merchants, ships

造中心。北京故宫、天坛、清东、西陵等皇家古建筑群就是以临清贡砖建造的。

位于临清市内运河西岸的临清钞关始建于明宣德四年（1429年），至今已有570余年的历史，在运河漕运史上占有极其重要的地位。"钞关"是明清朝廷在内河航线上设立的船税征收机构，大运河上共有钞关8处，临清就是其中之一。至明代万历年间，临清钞关每年征

and vehicles, and together in this place there are 32 commercail streets and 72 entertainment venus".

Linqing was not only an important commercial center, but also the largest royal brick kiln center of that time. The ancient royal architectural complexes like the Forbidden City, the Temple of Heaven, the East and West Tombs and so on were all built on bricks from Linqing.

The Linqing *Chaoguan* on the west canal bank was built 570 years ago in

● 临清钞关旧址（图片提供：FOTOE）
Former Site of Linqing *Chaoguan*

收的商税达到白银八万余两，居八大钞关之首。

临清的饮食文化别具风格，风味独特，其中最著名的要数托板豆腐和临清汤。托板豆腐也叫"水豆腐"，其最大特点是白嫩、细腻、香甜。托板豆腐被商贩切成一块块排在木制托板上，吃客付了钱，不加任何作料，端起木板将豆腐吸溜着倒进嘴里，其清香的味道令人满口生津。

1429, and was extremely important in the history of the grain shipping by canal. *Chaoguan* was the ship tax collection agency set up on the inland waterways by the courts of the Ming and Qing dynasties. There were 8 *Chaoguan* on the Grand Canal in total, and one of them sat in Linqing. By the Wanli Period of the Ming Dynasty, the Linqing *Chaoguan* had been able to collect commercial tax of 80 thousand taels of silver per year, which was the most among all the eight *Chaoguan*.

The catering culture of Linqing is also distinctive, and Plate Tofu and Linqing Soup are the most famous. The Plate Tofu is also called "Water Tofu", which is smooth, exquisite and dulcet. The peddler cut the tofu into pieces and put it on the wood plate. After paying money, the customer holds up the plate and sucks the tofu into a mouth without any condiment. The taste of sweetness is unforgettable.

## > 济宁

济宁市位于山东省西南部，地处微山湖的北端。古运河从济宁城中贯穿而过。发达的水陆交通，繁荣的商业贸易，再加上丰富的资源，使济宁素有"江北小苏州"之

- 大汶口文化花叶纹小口彩陶壶（新石器时代）
Small Mouth Painted Pottery Pot with Flower-leaf Pattern from Dawenkou Culture (Neolithic Age)

## > Jining

Jining locates in southwest Shandong Province, north to the Weishan Lake. The ancient canal flowed through the downtown of Jining. The advanced land and water communication, prosperous commercial trade, and the abundant resources crowned Jining the name of "Small Suzhou to the North of the Yangtze River". Early before six to seven thousand years ago, numerous primitive villages had been scattered in Jining region, including the famous Dawenkou Neolithic cultural site. During the Spring and Autumn Period and Warring States Period, this region became the birth place of the Confucianism for the born of Confucius, Mencius and other thinkers, and has been crowned the "Homeland of Confucius and Mencius" till now. During the reign of the Emperor Yang of Sui, the Grand Canal was excavated to the

大运河山东济宁段（图片提供：微图）
Jining Section of the Grand Canal in Shandong Province

称。早在六七千年前，济宁地区就散布着众多的原始村落，留下了许多古文化遗址，包括著名的大汶口新石器文化遗址。春秋战国时期，这一带以孔子、孟子等思想家的出现而成为儒家学说的发源地，至今以"孔孟之乡"闻名全国。隋炀帝时，大运河已经开挖至济宁地区，元代时运河又向北沟通京津，处于运河中段的济宁遂成为南北交通的咽喉。流经济宁城区的古运河段俗

Jining region. By the Yuan Dynasty, as the canal had stretched north to Beijing and Tianjin, Jining in the middle area of the canal became the strategic point of the north-south traffic. The ancient canal section flowing through Jining is commonly known as the "Grain Canal", and is 230 kilometers long in total. The three dynasties of Yuan, Ming and Qing all set up the Channel Governor-general Office, which was the top department of shipping agency, in Jining, provided

称"运粮河",全长约230千米。元、明、清三朝均在济宁设有最高司运机构,使济宁成为声名显赫的"运河之都"。明清时期的济宁码头帆樯如林,货物堆积如山,每年经此调往北方的粮食约占全国水运总量的三分之一,而且北方的毛皮、南方的瓷器和竹器以及周边地区的农副产品也在此地集散,济宁城内因此出现了鳞次栉比的商铺作坊。

it with the outstanding reputation of the "City of Canal". The wharfs in Jining during the Ming and Qing dynasties were piled with ships and cargos, and one third of the nationwide grain shipping to the north by water per year should be transferred in this place. Meanwhile, because Jining was the distributing center of the furs from the north, porcelains and bamboo articles from the south, and the subsidiary agricultural products produced in surrounding areas, numerous stores

- 济宁曲阜孔府大成殿
Dacheng Hall of Confucius Mansion in Qufu City, Jining

济宁汶上南旺镇地处京杭大运河全线的海拔最高点,被称为"水脊",从此处向北的运河常因水浅难以通航。明初,工部尚书宋礼和当地水利专家白英修建了南旺分水坝,引汶上县北境的大汶河之水入运河,使南北过往船只得以顺利通过。

and workshops emerged side by side in Jining city.

The Nanwang Town in Wenshang County in Jining has the highest elevation in the Grand Canal basin, which is called the "Canal Spine". The section from this place to the north had usually been hard to pass due to the low water level. In the early Ming Dynasty, the minister of works Song Li and the local hydrauic expert Bai Ying managed the construction of the Nanwang Diversion Dam, which introduced the Dawen River from the north border of Wenshang County into the canal, enabling ships from the north and south to smoothly pass.

### 微山湖

微山湖位于山东济宁辖下的微山县,是山东省第一大淡水湖。由微山、昭阳、独山、南阳四个彼此相连的湖泊组成,所以又称"南四湖",四湖中以微山湖面积最大,所以习惯上统称"微山湖"。微山湖承纳了鲁、苏、皖、豫四省区来水,有40多条河水汇流湖中,京杭大运河纵贯全湖,是南下苏杭及北上京津的重要水道。微山湖景色优美,湖中遍植荷花,多达万亩。每至盛夏,湖面上花团锦簇,荷香四溢,沁人心脾,景象蔚为壮观,因而有"中国荷都"之名。

### Weishan Lake

The Weishan Lake locates in Weishan County governed by Jining in Shandong Province, and is the largest freshwater lake of Shandong. As the lake is composed of four connecting small lakes of Weishan, Zhaoyang, Dushan and Nanyang, it is also called the "Nansi Lake (Four Lakes in the South) ". And because Weishan is the largest among the four, people commonly called them the "Weishan Lake" in general. The Weishan Lake intakes over 40 rivers from 4 provinces of Shandong, Jiangsu, Anhui and Henan, and is cutting through by the Grand Canal. For that reason, the lake is an important water way connecting Beijing in the north and Hangzhou in the south. The scenery of the Weishan Lake is beautiful and lotus can be seen everywhere covering the lake. In summer the booming flowers and rich lotus fragrance are extremely impressive, and people praise the lake as the "Lotus Lake of China".

- 微山湖中的万亩荷花（图片提供：FOTOE）
  Endless Lotuses on Weishan Lake

## > 聊城

聊城位于山东西部平原地区，明代时称为"东昌府"，京杭大运河从城西部流过。聊城古船闸、码头、古桥等是运河上的重要水利和交通设施，也是运河漕运的重要实物见证。

由于京杭大运河聊城段南北落差较大，而且缺少水源补给，为了确保运河畅通，元、明、清三代相继在这段河道上兴建了三十余处船闸，因此这段河流也被称为"闸河"。目前保留下来的八座船闸中，以周店闸保存最为完整。周店闸位于东昌府区凤凰办事处周店村，原名周家店闸，始建于元大德四年（1300年），包括南闸、北闸和月河涵洞三部分，是运河上保存最为完整的复式船闸。这些船闸建

## > Liaocheng

Liaocheng lies on the west plain of Shandong Province, and was called "Dongchang Prefecture" during the Ming Dynasty. The Beijing-Hangzhou Grand Canal flows through the western city. The ancient ship locks, wharfs and bridges in Liaocheng were important water conservancy and traffic facilities, and meanwhile the physical witness of the developed grain canal-shipping.

Due to the huge north-south difference of level and the lack of water recharging in the Liaocheng section of the Grand Canal, the Ming and Qing dynasties continuously constructed over 30 ship locks on this section to assure the smooth traffic, and the section was also called the "Canal of Lock" as a result. Among the 8 reserved ship locks at present, the Zhoudian Lock is the most complete, which locates in Zhoudian

• 聊城山陕会馆（图片提供：徽图）

聊城山陕会馆位于大运河西岸，是庙宇和会馆相结合的建筑群，于清乾隆八年（1743年）由山西、陕西两省的商人在这里合资兴建。会馆建筑规制严整，殿阁楼廊层檐飞动、线条流畅、彩绘绚丽，给人以富丽堂皇的感觉。

Shanxi-Shaanxi Guild Hall in Liaocheng

The Liaocheng Shanxi-Shaanxi Guild Hall lies on the west canal bank, is an architectural complex composed of temples and guildhalls, and was jointly built by the merchants from Shanxi and Shaanxi provinces in 1743. The constructions were built with neat regulation, smart design, smooth lines, and gorgeous color decorations, making an impression of magnificence.

Village in Dongchangfu District and was built in 1300 in the Yuan Dynasty. The lock was used to be named the Zhoujiadian Lock, and composed of three parts, the South Lock, North Lock and Yuehe Culvert. It's the most complete compound ship lock reserved on the canal. These ship lock buildings were reasonably structured and finely made, and have become the important materials for the study of the canal water conservancy and grain shipping development history.

During the Ming and Qing dynasties, many wharfs were built by the Liaocheng section of the Grand Canal for the handling of cargos. At the same time a lot of bridges were also constructed, among the most complete ones are North Bridge, Huitong Bridge, Yuejing Bridge and Wenjin Bridge. Besides, the numerous ancient constructions, dwellings, towns,

聊城古运河（图片提供：微图）
Ancient Canal in Liaocheng

筑结构合理，施工精细，是研究运河水利发展历史和漕运历史的重要实物资料。

明清时期，大运河聊城段的河道上建有许多码头，以供装卸货物。此外，还建有许多桥梁，目前保存较为完整的主要有北大桥、会通桥、月径桥、问津桥四座桥梁。

streets and so on scatterd by the canal are important for us to study the architectural art of all times and the history of grain shipping.

Being the gathering place of merchants and artists from all over the nation due to the canal, Liaocheng at that time was dotted with theaters, tea houses and clubs and inundated with numerous

此外，运河沿岸还散落着众多古建筑、古民居、古城镇、古街巷等，它们都是研究各时代建筑艺术、漕运历史的重要实物资料。

作为南北商人、艺人的集散地，当时的聊城戏园、茶肆、酒楼星罗棋布，南腔北调不绝于耳，无论是北方还是南方的剧种在聊城都有演出。同时，运河便利的交通为曲艺文化的南下北上提供了可能性，许多地方戏种、曲种在该地产生、传播、争奇斗艳。如山东快书、聊城八角鼓等就是源于聊城，后来流传于运河沿线城市，形成独特的曲艺文化。

dialects. Operas from no matter north or south were all performed in Liaocheng. At the same time, the convenient canal transportation provided possibility for the integration of the opera cultures, and many local operas emerged within the canal basin and were spread everywhere. For example, the Shandong Clapper Ballad and Liaocheng Octagonal Drum were originated from Liaocheng, then were spread to the cities by the canal, and formed the unique opera culture at last.

## > 淮安

　　淮安是位于江苏省中部偏北的一个城市，地处江淮平原的东部、淮河与京杭大运河的交汇点上，历史上与扬州、苏州、杭州并称大运河沿线的"四大都市"。

　　淮安境内绝大部分为辽阔的平原，地势平坦，而且河流湖泊众多，除了京杭大运河与淮河之外，西部还濒临中国第四大淡水湖洪泽湖，南部则有高邮湖、白马湖等。

　　早在夏商周时期，淮安就是南北交通枢纽。北宋以后直到元代，由于战争破坏和黄河夺淮的影响，淮安城曾经一度衰落。明代以后，随着漕运的兴盛，淮安城迎来再次繁荣。淮安不仅是漕运指挥中心，而且是漕船制造和漕粮转输的中心。当时两淮地区是全国最重要的

## > Huai'an

Huai'an locates on the eastern Yangze-Huaihe Plain, in the north of Jiangsu Province close to the central part, where the Huaihe River meets with the Grand Canal, and was one of the "Four Major Cities" by the canal together with Yangzhou, Suzhou and Hangzhou in the history.

　　Most territory of Huai'an consists of vast plains and has plenty of rivers and lakes. In addition to the Grand Canal and Huaihe River, there are the fourth largest freshwater lake Hongze Lake in the west, and the Gaoyou Lake, Baima Lake and so on in the south.

　　Early in the Xia, Shang and Zhou dynasties, Huai'an had been the north-south traffic hub. From the Northern Song to the Yuan dynasties, Huai'an declined for a time due to the warfare

● 淮安运河公园（图片提供：微图）
The Canal Park in Huai'an

盐区，而淮安就是淮北食盐的集散中心。与此同时，淮安又是粮船的盘验之处，每年经过这里的粮船有5000多只，随船人员达5万多人，除漕船官兵、水手、押运官员之外，还有众多的纤夫，再加上其他南来北往的人员，淮安流动人口多达十数万。在流动人口的拉动下，淮安的酿酒业、饮食业、客店业等获得很大发展。

由于地跨淮河两岸，淮安文化

and breaching of the Yellow River. By the Ming Dynasty, with the prosperous of the grain shipping, Huai'an had been developed once again, not only being the grain shipping command center, but also the ship construction and grain transferring center. The Huainan and Huaibei Region at that time were the major salt producing zone of the country, and Huai'an was the distribution center of the Huaibei Salt. Meanwhile, Huai'an was also a grain-ship check point dealing with

• 淮安总督漕运部院遗址 (图片提供：微图)

明清时期，朝廷在淮安设总督漕运部院衙门，以督查、催促南粮北调、北盐南运等工作。漕运总督的权力很大，不但管理漕运，还兼任巡抚。部院机构庞大，有文官武将及各种官兵达270多人，下辖储仓、造船厂、卫漕兵厂等。

### Grain Transportation Governor Office Relic in Huai'an

In the Ming and Qing dynasties, the court set up the Grain Transportation Governor in Huai'an to supervise and urge the south-north transportations of grain and the salt shipping from north to south. The power of the governor was huge, who not only controlled the grain shipping, but also held the concurrent post of the grand coordinator. The office was also big, with over 270 civil and military officers, and managed the storages, shipyards, weapon factories and so on facilities.

兼具北方与南方的文化风格。淮安历来就有"南船北马"之称，古时候，来自南方浙江、江西、福建等省的人，到了淮安下船登陆，换乘马车继续北上，而北方人也是在淮安弃车马坐船南下。淮安地区的民

over 5000 ships and 50 thousand crews per year. In addition to the officers, soldiers, sailors and escort personnel on the ships, there were also numerous ship trackers and personnel at all levels from all over the country. The hundreds of thousands of floating population promoted the development of the wine-making, catering, hospitality and so on industries of Huai'an.

Huai'an straddles on the Huaihe River, possessing both the north and south cultural styles, and has always been praised as "south boat and north horse". In ancient times, people from Zhejiang, Jiangxi, Fujian and so on provinces transferred from ships to horses in Huai'an and then set off again towards the north; the northerners also dismounted from the horses and boarded ships to the south in this city. The dwelling styles in Huai'an were also cut by the Huaihe River in two half. The constructions on the north bank were mainly quadrangle

居建筑，淮河以北的以土墙草盖的北方式四合院为主，而淮河以南则以青砖黛瓦的民居为主，具有典型的南方特征。

dwellings of the northern style, and the buildings on the south bank were built by blue bricks and black tiles with typical southern feature.

## 淮扬菜

淮扬菜指流行于江苏扬州、镇江、淮安及其附近地域的菜肴，与鲁菜、川菜、粤菜并称为中国四大菜系。淮扬菜选料严谨，讲究鲜活，主料突出，刀工精细，重视调汤，讲究原汁原味，并精于造型，口味咸淡适中。淮扬菜的著名菜肴有清炖蟹粉狮子头、大煮干丝、水晶肴肉等，菜品细致精美。

## Huaiyang Cuisine

The Huaiyang Cuisine refers to the dishes in Yangzhou, Zhenjiang, Huai'an and other regions of Jiangsu Province, and is collectively known as the Four Cuisines of China together with the Shandong Cuisine, Sichuan Cuisine and Guangdong Cuisine. The Huaiyang Cuisine emphasizes the material freshness, knife skills, main ingredients, soup bases, original flavor, modeling and moderate taste. The famous dishes are Stewed Crab Powder Pork Ball, Boiled and Dried Bean Curd, Salted Pork in Jelly and so on, which are exquisitely made.

- 淮扬名菜清炖狮子头

狮子头是将六成肥肉和四成瘦肉加上葱、姜、鸡蛋等配料斩成肉泥，做成拳头大小的肉丸，再用高汤清炖而成的，肥而不腻，入口即化。

### Famous Huaiyang Cuisine Stewed Pork Ball

The pork ball is made in fine streaky pork with green onion, ginger, eggs and other ingredients. First cut the raw materials into muddy flesh, then rub the fresh into meatballs in fist size, at last boil them with soup-stock. The mouth feel of this dish is fat but not greasy, just like balls melting in the mouth.

## > 扬州

　　扬州地处江苏省中部。大约距今7000—5000年前,扬州一带就已经有人类生活,并且开始了水稻的种植。春秋末年,吴国灭掉了扬州的邗国,筑邗城,并且开掘了连接长江、淮河两大水域的运河邗沟。现在扬州境内的运河与两千多年前的邗沟大部分重合,因此可以说扬州段的运河是整个大运河中最古老的一段。隋代大运河开通后,扬州成为运河上的水运枢纽,奠定了唐代扬州空前繁荣的基础。唐代的扬州,农业、商业和手工业相当发达,出现了大量的手工工场和作坊,不仅在江淮之间"富甲天下",而且成为中国东南第一大都会。在以长安(今陕西西安)为中心的水陆交通网中,扬州始终起着

## > Yangzhou

Yangzhou locates in the central area of Jiangsu Province. People exploited and grew rice in this region about 5000 to 7000 years ago. In the late Spring and Autumn Period, the State of Wu destroyed the Han Kingdom in Yangzhou. After that the State of Wu built the Hancheng and excavated the Hangou Canal connecting the Yangtze River and Huaihe River. As the canal within Yangzhou at present almost coincides with the Hangou Canal built over 2000 years ago, it can be said that the canal in Yangzhou is the oldest section of the Grand Canal. After the completion of the Grand Canal in the Sui Dynasty, Yangzhou became the water transportation hub, laying the foundation for its unprecedented prosperity in the Tang Dynasty. During the Tang Dynasty, the agriculture, business and handicrafts were pretty advanced, and vast handicraft

● 扬州"古邗沟"石碑（图片提供：全景正片）
Stele Carved with Character "Ancient Hangou Canal" in Yangzhou

枢纽的骨干作用。日本遣唐使来扬州和高僧鉴真东渡日本，促进了中日两国的政治、经济、科学和文化之间的交流。今天扬州城内的运河两岸，留下了许多反映扬州古港、水利和城池建筑的遗址，如水斗门、龙首关、东关古渡等。

两宋时期，随着农业和手工业的迅速发展和商业的进一步繁荣，扬州再度成为中国东南部的经济、文化中心。著名的文学家欧阳修、

factories and workshops appeared. Yangzhou was not only the wealthiest city in the Yangtze-Huaihe Region, but also the largest city in southeast China. In the Chang'an-centric (today's Xi'an in Shaanxi Province) waterway network, Yangzhou played the part of the backbone hub. Being a major external port, Yangzhou was specially set up with the shipping officer to manage the foreign trade and friendly communications. The imperial Japanese embassies to China

- **扬州瘦西湖**

瘦西湖位于江苏省扬州市西北部，形状清瘦狭长，窈窕曲折，水面长约4千米，宽不及100米，故称"瘦西湖"。

**Slender West Lake in Yangzhou**

The Slender West Lake locates in northwest Yangzhou in Jiangsu Province, with slim and zigzag shape. As the lake is about 4 kilometers long, but less than 100 meters wide, people called it the Slender West Lake.

苏轼、秦观、姜夔、王令等人都曾在游览扬州后，留下了大量歌咏扬州风光旖旎、市井繁华的诗文名作，使扬州成为人们心目中的"人间天堂"。

明清时期，扬州经济发展加快，来扬州经商、传教、定居的外国人日渐增多。扬州手工业十分发达，出产的漆器、玉器、铜器、竹

came to Yangzhou and invited the eminent monk Jianzhen back to Japan, which enhanced the political, economic, scientific and cultural communications between the two countries. There are still many ancient wharfs, water conservancy and city relics reserved by the canal banks in Yangzhou, like the Shuidou Gate, Dragon-head Pass, Dongguan Old Ferry and so on.

木器具、刺绣品等都十分精美，行销全国乃至海外。清代的康熙、乾隆两位皇帝曾多次巡幸扬州，当时扬州出现空前的繁华，城市人口超

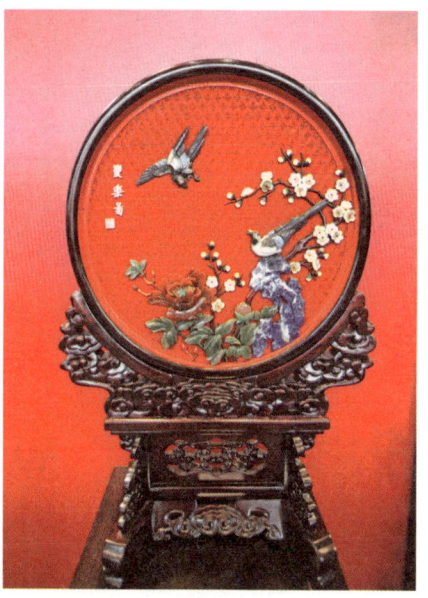

In the Song Dynasty, along with the rapid development of the agriculture and handicraft industries and the further prosperity of the economy, Yangzhou once again became the economic and cultural center in southeast China. Famous literati like Ouyang Xiu, Su Shi, Qin Guan, Jiang Kui, and Wang Ling, for example, visited Yangzhou and wrote vast masterpieces praising the beautiful scenery and prosperous marketplaces, making Yangzhou the "Heaven on Earth" in people's minds.

During the Ming and Qing dynasties, the economy of Yangzhou was well-developed, and more and more foreigners came to Yangzhou for business, preaching and immigration purposes. In the mean time, the handicraft industry in Yangzhou was also advanced. The lacquers, jade articles, bronze articles, bamboo articles, embroideries and cosmetics produced in the handicraft workshops reached a very high level and were sold all over the country and aboard. The emperors Kangxi and Qianlong of the Qing Dynasty used to visit Yangzhou many times, and the prosperity and population of Yangzhou reached its peak. During this period, the "Yangzhou Eight Elites" including the famous painters

- 扬州雕漆嵌玉双乐图台屏

雕漆是漆器工艺中的一个品种，即将生漆调成色漆一层层地涂在胚胎上，当达到一定厚度时，用刀在漆层上雕出各类图案纹样。扬州雕漆工艺始创于唐代，在明清时期达到顶峰，雕刻精致、刀法明快。作品线条流畅、色彩丰富、风格独特。

Yangzhou Lacquer Engraving Table Screen with Inlaid Jade Double-birds

The lacquer engraving is one of the lacquer handicrafts. Painted with raw lacquer onto the body in layers to a certain thickness at first, then carved the various patterns on the surface of the lacquer with a knife, a work has been done. The Yangzhou lacquer engraving craft originating in the Tang Dynasty reached its peak during the Qing Dynasty, and had delicate engraving, vivid cutting, smooth lines, lavish colors and unique style.

• **扬州个园**

清代，扬州的盐商开始营造园林，扬州至今还保留着许多优秀的古典园林，其中历史悠久、保存完整的要算坐落在古城北隅的个园。个园由两淮盐业商总黄至筠建于清嘉庆二十三年（1818年），园中景色以竹石取胜，园名中的"个"字是取"竹"字半边而来。

**Yangzhou Geyuan Garden**

The salt dealers from the Qing Dynasty started to build gardens in Yangzhou and many of the excellent ancient gardens have been reserved till today. Among which the most intact garden with the longest history is the Geyuan Garden sitting in the north of the early city. It was built by the Huainan & Huaibei salt industry leader Huang Zhiyun in 1818. The garden is famous for the bamboos, and the name "*Ge* (个)" was half the word "Bamboo (竹)" in Chinese.

过50万。这期间出现了以郑板桥、金农等著名画家为代表的"扬州八怪"及扬州画派，扬州的雕版印刷、民间曲艺、棋艺等均达到了全国最高的水平。

Zheng Banqiao and Jin Nong together with the Yangzhou Painting School appeared. The block printing, folk arts and chess art were the highest level over the country.

## > 镇江

镇江位于江苏省南部,长江三角洲北翼的中心,因扼守长江、地势重要,得名"镇江"。镇江还是

## > Zhenjiang

Zhenjiang locates in the eastern Jiangsu Province in the central area of the north Yangtze River Delta. Because of the important geographic location of guarding the Yangtze River, it got the name of "Zhenjiang" ("*Zhen*" refers to "garrison" in Chinese). And as the city sits in the meeting area of the Yangtze River and the Grand Canal

● **镇江金山寺佛塔** (图片提供:全景正片)

金山寺位于镇江市区西北。在民间传说《白蛇传》中,蛇精化成的美女白素贞为了救出被法海和尚困于金山寺中的丈夫许仙,曾大施法力,水漫金山。这也给古老的金山寺带来一抹浪漫的色彩。

**Pagoda in the Temple Jinshan in Zhenjiang**

Jinshan Temple locates in the northwest of Zhenjiang city. In the folk legend *The Legend of White Snake*, the beauty Bai Suzhen formed from a snake spirit used magic bringing flood to the Jinshan Temple for saving her husband Xu Xian who was trapped in the temple by Fahai Monk. The story provides the ancient Jinshan Temple with romantic mood.

长江与大运河交汇的枢纽，江南运河的起点，自古以来就是南北贸易的商埠重地。宋代时，太湖地区和钱塘江地区的漕粮、贡赋都是通过江南运河运至镇江，再转运至北方的，镇江成为王朝运输生命线上的咽喉。漕运的繁盛使镇江成为交通运输和商业贸易都非常繁荣的港口城市。在商贸运输业的刺激下，镇江的造船、冶炼、丝织等行业也得以兴旺发展，明代航海家郑和下西洋所用船只大多造于镇江。

and is the starting point of the Jiangnan Canal, it has always been the important commercial port for the north-south trading since antiquity. During the Song Dynasty, the grain and tributes from the Taihu Lake and Qiantang River regions shipping from the Jiangnan Canal to the north were transferred in Zhenjiang, where became the throat of the court's traffic lifeline. The prosperity of the grain shipping made Zhenjiang a harbor city with busy transportation and trading business, promoting the shipbuilding,

• 镇江市内大运河与长江交汇处（图片提供：FOTOE）
Meeting Point of the Grand Canal and the Yangtze River in Zhenjiang

● 《水漫金山》年画
New Year Picture: *Flooding the Jinshan Temple*

镇江自古人文荟萃。中国历史上第一部文学理论著作《文心雕龙》就是由南朝名士刘勰在这里撰写完成的。唐代著名诗人李白、骆宾王、孟浩然、刘禹锡、杜牧，宋代文学家苏轼、辛弃疾等人都曾在此留下传世之作。镇江民间还流传着《白娘子水漫金山》《梁红玉擂鼓战金山》等传说，这些脍炙人口的故事也为古城镇江增添了传奇色彩。

smelting, silk weaving and so on business in Zhenjiang. The ships used by Zheng He, the navigator of the Ming Dynasty, for the sailing to the West were mostly built in Zhenjiang.

Zhenjiang had gathered numerous scholars since ancient times. The first literary theory work of China *The Literary Mind and the Carving of Dragons* was written by the eminent person from the Southern dynasties Liu Xie in Zhenjiang. The famous poets of the Tang Dynasty including Li Bai, Luo Binwang, Meng Haoran, Liu Yuxi and Du Mu, and the poets from the Song Dynasty like Su Shi and Xin Qiji for example had all written down masterpieces in Zhenjiang. The folk legends like *The Flooding of Jinshan Temple Waged by White Snake, Liang Hongyu Beating Drum and Fighting in Jinshan Mountain* and so on have achieved universal praise and increased the legendary of this ancient town.

## > 无锡

无锡地处江苏省东南部，位于长江三角洲平原腹地，北倚长江，南临太湖，京杭大运河从城中穿过，自古就是中国著名的鱼米之乡和富庶之地。

无锡古运河的历史可以追溯到商末，周太王长子泰伯在梅里建勾吴国，为了灌溉和排洪的需要，就率领民众开凿了伯渎河。历史上吴王阖闾攻楚、吴王夫差北上伐齐都曾通过这条河。隋代京杭大运河全线贯通后，无锡运河在其中发挥了重要的作用。据史料记载，当时无锡的仓储大米每年都达到130万石以上，与湖南长沙、江西九江、安徽芜湖并称为"全国四大米市"。米市的兴旺也带动了无锡城其他行

## > Wuxi

Wuxi locates in southeast Jiangsu Province in the central Yangtze River Delta Plain, facing the Yangtze River in the north and the Taihu Lake in the south, and cut through by the Beijing-Hangzhou Grand Canal. It has always been the famous land of abundance of China since ancient times.

The history of the ancient canal in Wuxi can be traced back to the late Shang Dynasty, when Taibo, the eldest son of the King Tai of Zhou, established the State of Wu in Meili and managed the construction of the Bodu Canal for the irrigation and flood discharging needs. According to historical records, this canal was used by the King Helv of Wu to assault the State of Chu and the King Fuchai of Wu to crusade against

业的繁荣，据说当时无锡运河沿岸人来人往，商铺林立，各地客商云集，一片繁华景象。

市区古运河北端的河中有一座小岛，名叫黄埠墩。有人把流经无锡的运河比做一条龙，黄埠墩就是"龙头"。唐宋以来，黄埠墩就成为无锡运河中的一处胜迹。南宋末年的宰相文天祥被元

the State of Qi in the north. After the Emperor Yang of Sui fully completed the Beijing-Hangzhou Grand Canal, the Wuxi Canal played an important role in transportation, and together with Changsha in Hunan Province, Jiujiang in Jiangxi Province and Wuhu in Anhui Province became the "Four National Cities of Rice". According to historical materials, the rice storage in Wu of that

- **大运河无锡段河中的黄埠墩** (图片提供：全景正片)
  黄埠墩旧名"小金山"，墩小而圆，面积220平方米，四周是石砌驳岸。
  **Huangbudun in Wuxi Section of the Grand Canal**
  Huangbudun was used to be called the "Small Golden Hill", which is a small round islet of 220 square meters big and surrounded with stone revetment.

- **无锡惠山泥娃娃"大阿福"**

惠山泥人是产于无锡惠山的特色手工艺品，"大阿福"是惠山泥人中最具特色的作品。大阿福的造型是一个胖娃娃，脸型丰满，身穿锦袍，十分惹人喜爱。

**Huishan Clay Doll "Big Afu"**

The Huishan clay dolls are the local artifacts produced in Huishan Mountain region in Wuxi. Among which the "Big Afu" is the most distinctive work, which is an adorable chubby child wearing brocades.

军押往大都的途中，就被囚禁于黄埠墩。清代的康熙、乾隆两位皇帝数次南巡，每次都在墩上停留观赏，康熙帝把它比做水中的兰花，乾隆帝则称喻它是传说中的"蓬莱"。

运河为无锡孕育了独具特色的江南运河水乡文化。水弄堂是无锡最具特色的水乡风景。两边民居白墙黑瓦、高低错落，好一幅"人家尽枕河"的风情画。横跨在水弄堂

time could be over 1.3 million *Dan* every year. The thrifty rice trading promoted the other industries in Wuxi. It is said that the waterfront areas in Wuxi at that time were full of stores and merchants from all over the nation.

There is a small island in the middle of the ancient canal at the north end of the city called Huangbudun. If the canal in Wuxi is assimilated to a dragon, Huangbudun should be the "dragon head". Since the Tang and Song dynasties, Huangbudun had been a scenic spot of Wuxi. The minister Wen Tianxiang in the late Southern Song Dynasty was once imprisoned in Huangbudun by the Mongolian army as capture. The emperors Kangxi and Qianlong of the Qing Dynasty used to tour the south and stayed in Huangbudun for several times. Kangxi compared it with the orchid in the water, and Qianlong praised it as the legendary "Fairy Isle".

The canal bred the unique River South Water Culture for Wuxi, and the water alley is the most distinctive waterside view of Wuxi. The dwellings by rivers are made of white walls black tiles in different levels. It could be said that the house sleeps on the river. The Qingming Bridge crossing over the water

上的清明桥是无锡古运河上规模最大、保留最完整的单孔石拱桥，始建于明万历年间，至今已有400多年的历史。

alley is the largest and best reserved single-hole stone arch bridge on the ancient canal in Wuxi, and was built over 400 years ago in the Ming Dynasty.

- 无锡东林书院

东林书院创建于北宋政和元年（1111年），是当时北宋理学家程颢、程颐讲学的地方。明朝万历年间，著名学者顾宪成等人重新修复，并在此聚众讲学，东林书院一时声名鹊起，成为江南地区议论国事的舆论中心。

### Donglin Academy of Classical Learning in Wuxi

The Donglin Academy was established in 1111 in the Northern Song Dynasty, and was the teaching place of the philosophers Cheng Hao and Cheng Yi in the Northern Song Dynasty. In the Wanli Period in the Ming Dynasty, the famous scholars including Gu Xiancheng repaired this place and gave lectures here, greatly boosted its reputation and made it the major consensus center in the River South Region of that time.

## > 苏州

　　苏州位于江苏省的东南部，公元前6世纪，吴王阖闾建设吴都阖闾大城，是苏州建城之始，距今已有2500多年历史。隋开皇九年（589年）始称苏州，并一直沿用至今。苏州城建城早、规模大，至今保持着古代"水陆并行、河街相邻"的棋盘式格局。

　　今天的苏州段运河，北起与无锡接壤的望亭镇五七桥，穿过苏州市区，南至江苏与浙江交界的油车墩，全长96千米，约占江南运河长度的24%。苏州段运河最早开凿于公元前6世纪伍子胥主持建筑阖闾城时期，设水、陆城门各八座，外有护城河包围，内有水道相连。公元前495年，吴王夫差为北上争霸，下令开挖了一条人工河道，自今天的

## > Suzhou

Suzhou locates in southeast Jiangsu Province. In the 6th century B.C. about 2500 years ago, the King Helv of Wu established the capital Helv City, started the history of Suzhou. Since 589 in the Sui Dynasty, the city had been renamed Suzhou till now, which has a long history and large scale. The chessboard type city pattern of "water-land combining" is still reserved up to now.

　　The canal of the Suzhou section in nowadays starts from the Wuqi Bridge in Wangting Town bordering on Wuxi in the north to Youchedun at the bordering area of Jiangsu and Zhejiang provinces in the south, flowing across the downtown of Suzhou. The section is 96 kilometers long, accounting for 24% of the Jiangnan Canal. The canal of the Suzhou section was first excavated in the 6th century B.C.

- 苏州吴门桥

吴门桥位于苏州城西南隅的盘门外，地处运河与大龙江的交汇处，是苏州通往太湖的必经之道。此桥始建于北宋元丰七年（1084年），全长66.3米，桥面宽5米，拱高9.5米，以苏州金山花岗岩构筑，杂有少量宋代旧桥所遗的武康石。

Wumen Bridge in Suzhou

The Wumen Bridge locates outside the Panmen Gate in southwest Suzhou in the junction area of the canal and Dalong River, was built in 1084 and the only route from Suzhou to the Taihu Lake. The bridge is 66.3 meters long, 5 meters wide and 9.5 meters high, and was constructed by granite from Jinshan Mountain in Suzhou together with a small quantity of the Wukang Stone left from the old bridge built in the same dynasty.

苏州经无锡至常州与孟河连接，可达长江，此为江南运河最早开挖的河段。7世纪初，隋炀帝下令在已有水道的基础上开凿江南运河，从镇

when Wu Zixu managed the construction of the Helv City, and was set up with eight water gates and eight land gates. Meanwhile, there was a city moat surrounding and interconnected water channels within the city. In 495 B.C., for the expedition of the north, the King Fuchai of Wu gave orders to excavate a manmade channel from today's Suzhou to Changzhou, flowing through Wuxi and connecting the Menghe River. The channel could reach the Yangtze River, and was the earliest section of the Jiangnan Canal. In the early 7th century, the Emperor Yang of Sui commanded the

- 苏州出产的碧螺春茶

碧螺春茶原产于苏州洞庭东山，原名"吓煞人香"，清代康熙帝南巡时尝过此茶，赐名"碧螺春"。其成茶茶叶蜷曲似螺，边沿有一层均匀的细白绒毛，冲泡后清香袭人，且带有特殊的果香，是中国"十大名茶"之一。

**Spring Spiral Tea Produced in Suzhou**

The Spring Spiral Tea originates from the east Dongting Mountain in Suzhou and was used to be called the "Fearful Fragrance". The Emperor Kangxi of Qing used to taste this tea when touring the south and gave it the name of "Spring Spiral". It's one of the ten great teas of China, the leaves shape like fuzzy spirals and the boiled tea smells like the spring with special aroma.

江至杭州，长约400千米，河面宽约33.3米。苏州古城段的运河作为江南运河的重要区段，自此正式纳入大运河水系。

江南运河修成后，因苏州古城以南地势低下，没有陆路，汛期一至，河湖不分。9世纪初，苏州刺史王仲舒在太湖东缘修筑了一条长堤，将太湖与运河分开，同时在太湖的泄水口澹台湖与运河之间建造了宝带桥，解决了运

excavation of the Jiangnan Canal from Zhenjiang to Hangzhou based on the foundation of the existing channels. The canal was about 400 kilometers long and over 33 meters wide. As a major part of the Jiangnan Canal, the ancient canal of the Suzhou section had been officially absorbed by the Grand Canal water system since then.

After the completion of the Jiangnan Canal, as the south Suzhou ancient town was low-lying without land route, the rivers and lakes mixed together in rainy seasons. In the early 9th century, Wang Zhongshu, the governor of Suzhou, built a long dyke along the east edge of the Taihu Lake, separating the Taihu Lake with the canal. Meanwhile he constructed the Baodai Bridge between the Tantai Lake, which was the discharge opening of the Taihu Lake, and the canal, resolved the canal shipping issue. This section of canal was called the Wujiang Water Route in the history and had been repaired for several times in the later dynasties. Till today, the section is still plenty in water source, stable in channel and smooth in traffic.

For the reinforcing of the connection between the canal and ancient Suzhou city, in 825, the great poet Bai Juyi who

河航运的风险，史称吴江塘路，以后历代均有多次修缮。直至今天，该段运河依然水源充沛、航道稳定、运输通畅。

为了加强运河与苏州古城的联系，唐代宝历元年（825年），时任苏州刺史的大诗人白居易在虎丘

was the governor of Suzhou at that time excavated a channel from today's Huqiu by the Shantang River to the moat at the Changmen Gate, and constructed a dyke along the channel as road called the Baigong Dyke. As this channel connected the natural channels of the Baiyang Bay and the canal, the Shantang River

• 苏州盘门水城门

过吴门桥不远就是盘门，它是苏州现存最古老的一座城门，也是中国现存陆城门和水城门并存的唯一一座城门。离此不远处，还耸立着北宋时期修建的瑞光塔。吴门桥建成后，和盘门、瑞光塔一起，构成了苏州市西南部著名的"盘门三景"。

Panmen Water Gate in Suzhou

The Panmen Gate closing to the Wumen Bridge is the oldest city gate reserved in Suzhou and the only land-water integrated gate reserved in China. Near this gate, there is the Ruiguang Tower built in the Northern Song Dynasty. The Wumen Bridge, Panmen Gate and Ruiguang Tower constitute the famous "Three Views of Panmen" in southwest Suzhou.

至阊门护城河间开凿渠道,即今天山塘河的虎丘至阊门段,并沿河筑堤为路,人称"白公堤"。由于这一河段与西北边白洋湾的天然河道相通,直达运河,因此山塘河成为大运河北入苏州城的一条重要水道。唐代张继的千古名作《枫桥夜泊》就描绘了诗人夜半乘船从山塘河来到苏州城外寒山寺的情景:"月落乌啼霜满天,江枫渔火对愁眠。姑苏城外寒山寺,夜半钟声

became an important water route for the Grand Canal entering into Suzhou. The masterpiece *Mooring by Maple Bridge at Night* by Zhang Ji of the Tang Dynasty mentioned the scene of the writer coming from the Shantang River to Hanshan Temple outside Suzhou by boat in the midnight, "Moon's down, crows cry and frost fills all the sky; by maples and boat lights, I sleepless lie. Outside Suzhou Hanshan Temple is in sight; its ringing bells reach my boat at midnight." This

• 苏州山塘街的水乡风光
Waterside Scenery of Shantang Street in Suzhou

• 苏菜名品——松鼠桂鱼
Famous Suzhou Dish "Sweet and Sour Mandarin Fish"

到客船。"这首诗同时也记录了一个史实：最迟在公元8世纪，山塘河已与大运河及苏州古城水系贯通，四方客船通过山塘河可以抵达城外枫桥。

苏州气候温润，适宜各种动植物生长，因此饮食资源非常丰富。自春秋时起，吴国贵族就过着钟鸣鼎食、甘脂膏粱的奢华生活。秦汉到明清时期，苏州一直是封建王朝皇室内廷的食物供应基地之一，香粳米、洞庭红橘、碧螺春茶等特产都成为皇家贡品。千百年来，苏州饮食形成了独特的风格，有苏式菜肴、糕点、糖果、卤菜、蜜饯、糕团、名茶、炒货、调味品、酱菜等诸多品种。

poem also recorded a historical fact, that by the 8th century at latest, the Shantang River had already connected with the Grand Canal and the water system in ancient Suzhou city, and ships could reach the Maple Bridge outside the city through the Shantang River.

The mild climate in Suzhou fits for the growth of various plants and animals, and the food resources are plenty as a result. Early in the Spring and Autumn Period, the nobles in the State of Wu had lived a lush life. From the Qin and Han dynasties to the Ming and Qing dynasties, Suzhou had always been one of the food supply bases of the feudal royal courts. The endemic Xiangjing Rice, Dongting Red Orange, Spring Spiral Tea and so on were all paid to the courts as tributes. For thousands of years, the diet in Suzhou has formed its own style, including many varieties of Suzhou dishes, pasties, candies, pot-stewed meat or fowl, glace fruit, rice cakes, tea, roasted seeds and nuts, condiment, pickled vegetable and so on.

## 苏州园林

　　苏州古典园林的历史可上溯至公元前6世纪春秋时吴王的苑囿，而最早见于记载的私家园林是东晋名士顾辟疆所建的辟疆园。明清时期，苏州成为中国最繁华的地区之一，全盛时有园林200余处。苏州园林吸收了中国古典园林建筑艺术的精华，在构筑园景时因地制宜，以借景、对景、分景、隔景等多种手法来组织空间，造成园林中曲折多变、小中见大、虚实相间的艺术效果。通过叠山理水、栽植花木、配置园林建筑，使园林充满诗情画意的文人情怀。拙政园、留园、狮子林、沧浪亭、环秀山庄、艺圃、耦园、网师园、退思园等9座园林已被列入《世界遗产名录》，世界遗产委员会评价："这些建造于11—19世纪的园林，以其精雕细琢的设计，折射出中国文化中取法自然而又超越自然的深邃意境。"

- **苏州拙政园香洲**
  拙政园是苏州园林中面积最大的山水园林。香洲是园中的标志性景观之一，为典型的"舫"式结构，有两层舱楼，通体高雅。
  Boat-like Structure in Suzhou Humble Administrator's Garden
  The Humble Administrator's Garden is the largest Chinese landscape garden among the Suzhou Gardens, and the Boat-like Structure is one of the landmarks of it. The Boat-like Structure is in classic boat-type shape and has two floors, and the style is elegant and smart.

## Suzhou Gardens

The history of the classic garden in Suzhou can be traced back to the gardens of the State of Wu in the Spring and Autumn Period in 6th century B.C., and the first private garden to be recorded was the Pijiang Garden built by Gu Pijiang who was a scholar of the Eastern Jin Dynasty. During the Ming and Qing dynasties, Suzhou became one of the most prosperous places of China, and had over 200 gardens at most. The Suzhou Gardens absorbed the essence of the Chinese classic garden architectural art, and could adjust measures to local conditions when constructing the view of the garden, creating the ever-changing artistic effect, which could be seemingly false and real at the same time. By the configuration of the rockeries, water, plants and the garden structures, the gardens had been endowed with literary and artistic breath. The 9 gardens of the Humble Administrator's Garden, Lingering Garden, Lion Grove Garden, Pavilion of Surging Waves, Mountain Villa with Embracing Beauty, Garden of Cultivation, Couple's Retreat Garden, Master of the Nets Garden and Retreat and Reflection Garden had been enrolled into "The World Heritage List". The World Heritage Committee appraised these gardens built from the 11th to 19th centuries as "reflect the profound metaphysical importance of natural beauty in Chinese culture in their meticulous design".

- 苏州狮子林

狮子林建于元末明初，布局紧凑，素以假山著称。园中假山多且气势磅礴、玲珑俊秀、洞壑盘旋，就像一座曲折迷离的大迷宫。

### Lion Grove Garden in Suzhou

The Lion Grove Garden built during the late Yuan and early Qing dynasties is in compact distribution and famous for the numerous, magnificent and delicate rockeries bestrewed with holes, just like a twist and blurred giant labyrinth.

## > 嘉兴

嘉兴市位于浙江省东北部、长江三角洲杭嘉湖平原腹心地带，是长江三角洲重要城市之一。春秋战国时期，嘉兴是吴越两国争战之地，秦时置县，称"由拳"。三国吴时，由拳有"野稻自生"，吴主孙权将其更名为"禾兴"，后改称"嘉兴"。两晋南北朝时，嘉兴得到进一步开发，农业得到很大发展。隋朝开凿江南河，由杭州经嘉兴到镇江，给嘉兴带来灌溉、舟楫之利。唐代，嘉兴已成为中国东南重要的产粮区，有"嘉禾一穰，江淮为之康"的说法。宋元时，嘉兴经济飞速发展，手工业尤其发达，被称为"百工技艺与苏杭等"，而且商品经济日渐繁荣。嘉兴出产的棉布、丝绸行销南北，远至海外，

## > Jiaxing

Jiaxing locates in northeast Zhejiang Province in the core region of the Hangjiahu Plain, and is one of the major cities of the Yangtze River Delta. Jiaxing was the battle field between the states of Wu and Yue in the Spring and Autumn Period, and became a county called Youquan during the Qin Dynasty. In the Three Kingdoms Period, as wild rice grew in Youquan, the King Sun Quan of Wu renamed it Hexing (means the place of rice in Chinese) at first, then called it Jiaxing later. In the Wei, Jin, Northern and Southern dynasties, Jiaxing was further developed, especially for the agriculture industry. The Jiangnan Canal excavated by the Sui Dynasty from Hangzhou to Zhenjiang brought Jiaxing the benefits of irrigation and transportation. By the Tang Dynasty, Jiaxing had become the important grain-

● 浙江嘉兴段大运河岸边的三塔（图片提供：FOTOE）
Three Towers Standing by Jiaxing Section of the Grand Canal in Zhejiang Province

闻名遐迩。至明代，嘉兴已有"江东一大都会"的美誉。

　　江南运河嘉兴段北起王江泾镇，南到桐乡崇福镇，全长81.22千米。因地处水乡，沿河风光秀丽，现在已成为一条广受欢迎的水上观光线。嘉兴城西运河三塔湾的河畔，耸立着三座砖塔，被人们称为"嘉兴三塔"。这三座塔

producing zone in southeast China, and was praised as "mother of the Yangtze-Huaihe Region". During the Song and Yuan dynasties, the economy in Jiaxing was well developed, especially for the handicraft industry, which enjoyed equal popularity against the Suzhou and Hangzhou. And the commodity economy was also prosperous. The silk and cotton produced in Jiaxing were sold all over the country and aboard. By the Ming Dynasty, Jiaxing had been crowned

最早建于唐代，运河到三塔这里要经过一个急转弯，水流湍急。相传唐代高僧行云云游到此，见此处水深流急，为避免舟船翻覆，就运土填潭，并建起三座塔，以"镇潭中白龙"。现在的三塔为1999年重建，均为七层，中间最高的一座15米，塔为实心，每层都有佛龛。其实这三座塔也相当于运河中的航标，过去船工水手远远望

the "One of Metropolis of the Left Yangtze River Basin".

The Jiaxing section of the Jiangnan Canal starts from Wangjiangjing Town in the south to Chongfu Town in Tongxiang City in the south, and is 81.22 kilometers long. For the beautiful water-land scenery, it has become a popular water sightseeing line. There are three brick towers standing by the Three Tower Bend of the west canal of Jiaxing called the "Three Towers in Jiaxing", which

- 嘉兴古镇西塘的水乡风光
  Water-land Scenery in Ancient Xitang Town in Jiaxing

见三塔，就会小心行驶。现在三塔已成为嘉兴乃至整个京杭大运河的标志物。

- **嘉兴粽子**

粽子是一种用粽叶包裹糯米蒸制而成的小吃，也是嘉兴传统名点，以糯而不糊、肥而不腻、香糯可口、咸甜适中而著称，尤以鲜肉粽最为出名。

**Jiaxing Rice-pudding**

The rice-pudding is made in sticky rice packing in bamboo leaves, and is a traditional snack of Jiaxing. It's widely known for the mouth feel of sticky but not pasty and meanwhile fat but not greasy, and the delicious moderate taste. Among all the flavors the fresh meat rice-pudding is the most famous.

were firstly built in the Tang Dynasty. The canal takes a sudden turn in this place with turbulent flow. According to the legend, Xingyun, the eminent monk in the Tang Dynasty, passed this place and saw the turbulent water flowing through the Three Tower Bend. To avoid the ships from capsizing, he managed the river reclamation and the construction of the Three Towers. The towers at present were rebuilt in 1999, each of them has seven floors, and the highest one in the middle is 15 meters tall. The towers are solid, and on each floor there is a niche. Actually, the Three Towers can be seen as the navigation marks of the canal. In the past, when sailors saw the towers, they would slow the ship down. By now the Three Towers have become the landmarks of Jiaxing, and even of the entire Grand Canal.

### 嘉兴南湖

嘉兴市南面的南湖素来以"轻烟拂渚"的景色著称于世。湖中有两个岛屿，一为湖心岛，一为小瀛洲。湖心岛位于南湖中心，以烟雨楼为主体的古园林建筑群便坐落于此。烟雨楼始建于五代时期，至今已有1000多年的历史。烟雨楼重檐画栋、朱柱明窗，登楼远眺，景色可尽收眼底。楼内保存着大量文人学士留下的字碑石刻，具有相当高的文物价值。小瀛洲位于南湖东北部，清代时由淤泥堆积而成，俗称"小南湖"。1921年7月23日，中国共产党第一次全国代表大会在上海法租界秘密召开。会议进行至中途，遭法租界巡捕的袭扰，被迫转移到嘉兴南湖的一条游船上继续进行。南湖岸边至今还停泊着一条仿制游船，以纪念当年的事件。

## The South Lake in Jiaxing

The South Lake in southern Jiaxing is famous for its dimly discernible scenery. There are two islets in the lake, the Mid-lake Islet and Lesser Yingzhou. The Mid-lake Islet lies in the center of the South Lake, and is set up with the Pavilion of Mist and Rain based ancient garden architectural complex. The Pavilion of Mist and Rain was built around 940 in the Five dynasties over 1000 years ago, and is constructed with double-hipped roofs, painted rafters, red pillars and bright windows. Climbing up the high building and looking out, one could have a panoramic view. Meanwhile, there are vast proper carved stones marked by the scholars of high cultural value reserved in the pavilion. The Lesser Yingzhou lies in the northeast lake, was piled up by sludge in the Qing Dynasty and is commonly called the "Lesser South Lake". On July 23, 1921, the first national congress of the communist party of China was secretly held in the French concession of Shanghai. The conference was disturbed by the police of the French concession and was forced to transfer onto a sightseeing boat on the South Lake in Jiaxing. There is still a imitative sightseeing boat rest by the South Lake to commemorate this event till today.

- 嘉兴南湖湖心岛（图片提供：FOTOE）
Mid-lake Islet in the South Lake in Jiaxing

## > 杭州

　　位于大运河最南端的杭州，东临钱塘江入海处，并与浙东运河相连。丰饶的物产、便利的水运，使杭州自古以来就是富饶的商业

• 杭州六和塔
Pagoda of Six Harmonies in Hangzhou

## > Hangzhou

Hangzhou lies in the south end of the Grand Canal, is close to the estuary of the Qiantang River in the east and connected with the East Zhejiang Canal. The productive materials and convenient water traffic have made it a rich commercial city since ancient times. As the saying goes, "Up above there is Paradise, down here there are Suzhou and Hangzhou."

　　The Gongchen Bridge locates north to the Daguan Bridge within the downtown of Hangzhou and stretches across the Grand Canal from east-west. It's the symbol of the Grand Canal's destination and the longest stone arch bridge among all the ancient bridges in Hangzhou. The Gongchen Bridge was built in 1631 by a provincial graduate called Zhu Huafeng, who raised money for the construction. The bridge collapsed

城市，俗话说"上有天堂，下有苏杭"。

拱宸桥位于浙江杭州市内的大关桥之北，东西横跨大运河，是京杭大运河到杭州的终点标志，也是杭州古桥中最高、最长的石拱桥。拱宸桥始建于明崇祯四年（1631年），由当时一个名叫祝华封的举人募集资金建造。清顺治八年（1651年），桥因故坍塌，康熙五十三年（1888年）得以重修。在古代，"宸"是指帝王居住之所，

collapse in 1651 and was rebuilt in 1888 during the Kangxi Period. In ancient Chinese language, "*Chen*" referred to the living place of the emperor and "*Gong*" meant respect. Thus the name "Gongchen Bridge" referred to the meaning of respect to the emperor who toured the south. The bridge is 98 meters long, 16 meters tall, slightly narrow in the middle, and 12.2 meters wide in the both ends. The bridge body is made in boulder strips, the bridge surface is in soft arc-shape, and the pier is thin with three holes. The appearance

● 杭州运河上的拱宸桥 （图片提供：微图）
Gongchen Bridge Crossing the Canal in Hangzhou

• 风光旖旎的杭州西湖
Beautiful West Lake in Hangzhou

"拱"即两手相合表示敬意。"拱宸桥"的桥名代表了皇帝南巡时对皇帝的相迎和尊崇之意。桥长98米,高16米,桥面中段略窄,而两端桥塊处有12.2米宽。桥身用条石砌筑,桥面呈柔和的弧线形,桥下为三孔薄墩,桥形巍峨高大,气魄雄伟。

离拱宸桥不远,还有一座著名

of the bridge is eminent and magnificent.

Close to the Gongchen Bridge, there is another famous ancient bridge called the River-rising Bridge, which had been recorded in historical books early since the Northern Song Dynasty. According to the legend, when the tidal bore of Qiantang River came, the dense fog and cloud would spread all over this place, and the bridge got its name from that. Near the Gongchen Bridge, there also lied the largest granary at that time, the Fuyi Granary, which enjoyed equal popularity with the Nanxincang Granary in Beijing. Together, they were called the "Granaries of the World", and people praised them as the "Nanxincang Granary in the north and Fuyi Granary in the south". The Fuyi Granary built in 1880, had 50 to 60 storages in the past, and each of which was 20 square meters big and could store 40 to 50 thousand *Dan* of grain. This granary is the grain distribution center of Hangzhou and the

• 今天的余杭运河
Today's Yuhang Canal

的古桥，叫做江涨桥。早在北宋时期，此桥就在史书中有记载。据说，钱塘江的大潮来临时，大雾漫天，云气涨满，一直漫到此地而得名。在拱宸桥附近，还有当时最大的粮仓——富义仓。它与北京的南新仓并称"天下粮仓"，有"北有南新仓，南有富义仓"之说。富义仓始建于清光绪六年（1880年），当时仓内共有五六十间粮仓，每间

transfer station of the south-north grain transportation.

The Pagoda of Six Harmonies stands on the Moon Peak in Hangzhou on the north bank of the Qiantang River, and is jointly called the "Four Towers of the Canal" together with the Dipamkara Pagoda in Tongzhou, Wenfeng Pagoda in Yangzhou and Linqing Stupa. The place where the Pagoda of Six Harmonies sits was the garden belonging to the

约20平方米，可存四五万石谷物。这里是杭州各地粮食的集中地，也是南粮北运的中转站。

六和塔坐落在杭州钱塘江北岸的月轮峰上，与通州燃灯古塔、扬州文峰塔、临清舍利塔并称"运河四大名塔"。六和塔所在地原来是五代时吴越国主的南果园，公元970年，吴越国主钱弘俶为了镇压钱塘江的大潮，在此地舍园造塔，除了六和塔之外，同时建造的还有雷峰塔和保俶塔。据说建塔之后，钱塘江潮果然不再肆虐。六和塔塔身共9层，高近60米，伟岸挺拔，气魄非凡。塔的顶层装有明灯，可为夜晚航行的船只指引方向。

大运河的开通成就了杭州湖墅

King of the Wuyue Kingdom in the Five dynasties. In 970, the King Qian Hongchu of Wuyue abandoned the garden for the construction of the Pagoda to suppress the tidal bore of Qiantang River. In addition to this pagoda, the Leifeng Pagoda and Baochu Pagoda were all in construction at the same time. According to the legend, after the completion of the pagoda, the tidal bore of Qiantang River really ceased. The Pagoda of Six Harmonies had 9 floors nearly 60 meters high, with magnificent momentum. The top floor was equipped with beacon, which could navigate for the ships sailing at night.

The completion of the Grand Canal brought prosperity to the Hushu Region in Hangzhou and bred the unique canal-

● **杭州名菜西湖醋鱼**

杭州菜属中国八大菜系之浙菜，清爽别致是其最大的特点。其中，西湖醋鱼、东坡肉、吴山酥油饼等名扬中外。

**Famous Hangzhou Dish "West Lake Vinegar Fish"**

The Hangzhou Cuisine resides to the Zhejiang Cuisine, which is one of the Eight Cuisines of China, and the biggest characteristic of the Hangzhou Cuisine is fresh and chic. Dishes such as the West Lake Vinegar Fish, Dongpo's Pork, Wushan Hill Crisp Cake and so on are well-known both at home and abroad.

地区的繁荣，也令此地形成了运河沿岸特有的民间艺术和民间习俗。在湖墅一带，至今有曲艺、杂技、魔术、皮影戏等多种民间艺术形式流传。逢年过节，这里还有运河龙舟赛、桑秧会、河畔灯会、祈蚕等活动。

style folk art and custom, including the local musical theaters, acrobatics, magic, shadow play and so on folk forms of art, and the canal dragon boat race, mulberry festival, lantern show, silkworm praying and so on activities held on New Year's Day or other festivals.

## 西湖十景
## Ten Views of West Lake

在以西湖为中心的49平方千米的风景区内，分布有40多处名胜，其中以"西湖十景"最为著名。

Within the 49 square kilometers West Lake-centric scenic zone, there are over 40 places of interest. Among which the Ten Views of the West Lake are the most famous.

### 苏堤春晓

苏堤在西湖西侧，南北两端衔接南山路与北山路，是北宋诗人苏轼在杭州为官时组织民工开浚西湖、挖泥堆筑而成的。堤上有映波、锁澜等6座石拱桥，起伏相间，两边夹种桃树、柳树，风光旖旎。尤其是春天早晨，湖面薄雾，堤上烟柳，十分迷人。

### Spring Dawn on the Su Causeway

The Su Causeway locates to the west of the West Lake, connects to the South Mount Road in the south and North Mount Road in the north, and was constructed by Su Shi, the poet of the Northern Song Dynasty, with the sediment excavated from the dredging of the West Lake. There are 6 stone arch bridges including the Yingbo Bridge and Suolan Bridge scattering on the causeway. In spring, with the lakeside sparkling in the morning dew, birds cheerfully chirping among swaying willow branches, and the scent of peach blossoms wafting through the air, people will feel like in the midst of paradise.

### 柳浪闻莺

柳浪闻莺位于西湖东南岸，原为南宋皇帝的御花园，沿湖遍植垂柳，浓荫深处时时传来呖呖莺声，因而名为柳浪闻莺。

### Orioles Singing in the Willows

The spot locates on the southeast bank of the West Lake, and was an imperial garden built in the Southern Song Dynasty. Featuring green willows and singing orioles, the spot got its name.

### 曲院风荷

曲院风荷在苏堤北端的跨虹桥下，本是宋代酿造官酒的曲院，种满荷花，清香四溢。现在的曲院风荷成为一处布局精巧的小型园林，傍水建有廊、轩、亭、阁，古朴典雅。

● 西湖御码头附近的"柳浪闻莺"
Scene of "Orioles Singing in the Willows" Close to Royal Wharf in the West Lake

### Winery Yard and Lotus Pool

This scene locates beneath the Rainbow-crossing Bridge in the north end of the Su Causeway, and has earned its fame since the Song Dynasty, when the lakeside area with an abundant growth of lotus was known as Crooked Courtyard, and was a location of a brewery. At present there is an exquisite small garden in this place built with graceful corridors and pavilions.

### 平湖秋月

平湖秋月位于白堤西端，三面临水，背倚孤山。清康熙三十八年（1699年）在此建造御书楼，楼前挑出水面铺筑平台，题名为平湖秋月。皓月当空的秋夜，在平台上眺望西湖，景色非常美丽。

### Autumn Moon over the Calm Lake

This spot lies in the western end of the White Causeway, faces the mountain in one side, and the water in three sides. The Emperor Kangxi of the Qing Dynasty built a royal library with platform above the water in 1699, and etched the calligraphy as "Autumn Moon on Calm Lake". The platform is a special place to appreciate the moon in the fine autumn night.

三潭印月

三潭印月在西湖小岛小瀛洲南的水面上，有3座造型美丽的小石塔。每逢中秋夜，皓月当空，在塔内点上灯烛，洞口蒙上薄纸，灯光从中透出，宛如一个个小月亮倒映水中，三潭印月由此得名。

**Three Pools Mirroring the Moon**
On the south of the Lesser Yingzhou in the West Lake, there are three hollow stone pagodas rising from the water. In the night of Mid-Autumn Festival when the moon can be clearly seen, light the candles within the pagodas and cover the holes with thin paper, the light emanates out like many tiny moons reflecting in the water. So the spot got its name.

- 曲院风荷
Winery Yard and Lotus Pool

### 雷峰夕照

西湖南岸的夕照山上原有一座雷峰塔。夕阳西照时，塔影横空，金碧辉煌。1924年，雷峰塔倒塌，现在的雷峰塔为近年新建。

### Leifeng Pagoda in Evening Glow

On the Sunset Mountain on the south bank of the West Lake there was used to stand the Leifeng Pagoda, which was extremely resplendent and magnificent in the shining of the setting sun. The pagoda collapsed in 1924 and the one at present was newly constructed in recent years.

### 南屏晚钟

南屏晚钟是指南屏山下净慈寺的钟声。净慈寺始建于公元954年，是西湖四大丛林寺院之一。寺前原有一口大钟，每到傍晚，钟声响起，晚景十分迷人。

"三潭印月"的小石塔
Pagoda of "Three Pools Mirroring the Moon"

### Evening Bell Ringing at the Nanping Hill

This spot refers to the bell ring from the Jingci Temple down the Nanping Hill. The Jingci Temple was built in 954 and is one of the Four Temples of the West Lake. There was used to be a big bell in the temple and rang every dusk, when the scenery was very charming.

### 断桥残雪

断桥是白堤的东起点，正处于外湖和北里湖的分水点上，中国民间传说《白蛇传》的故事就发生在这里。旧时石拱桥上有台阶，桥中央有小亭，冬日雪霁，桥上向阳面冰雪消融，阴面却留有残雪，桥面看上去似断非断，景观奇特。

### Lingering Snow on the Broken Bridge
The Broken Bridge is the east starting point of the White Causeway, lies on the boundary of the outer lake and inner lake, is where the famous Chinese folk tale *The Legend of the White Snake* happened. In old times, there were footsteps and a small pavilion in the middle of the bridge. After a snowfall, when the snow on the more exposed side has melted, with the shade side remaining white, it looks as if a long white belt has been ripped apart.

### 双峰插云
双峰插云位于灵隐路上的洪春桥边。"双峰"指的是天竺山环湖山脉中的南高峰、北高峰。两峰遥相对峙，山雨欲来时，双峰的峰尖插入云端、忽隐忽现，十分壮观。

### Twin Peaks Piercing the Clouds
This spot locates by the Hongchun Bridge on Lingyin Road. The "Twin Peaks" refers to the South Peak and North Peak of the Tianzhu Mountains. On a drizzling day, the two peaks come and go amongst drifting rain and clouds, the scene is spectacular.

### 花港观鱼
花港观鱼位于苏堤南端。古代，有小溪自花家山流经此处入西湖，所以称花港。宋时，花家山下建有卢园，园内栽花养鱼，风光如画，被画家标上花港观鱼之名。现已建成大型公园，游人围拢鱼池投饵，群鱼翻腾水面，鱼乐人也乐。

### Viewing Fish at Flower Pond
The Flower Pond lies in the south end of the Su Causeway, and got its name for the small river came from the Flower Mountain flowing into the West Lake in this place in ancient time. In the Song Dynasty, there was a garden called Luyuan at the foot of Flower Mountain, and was labeled "Viewing Fish at Flower Pond" by painters for the beautiful scene of the flowers and fishes in the garden. Till today, the place has been built into a large park, where people can enjoy the sight of brightly colorful fish swimming around and feed them. To stay with nature is a highly enjoyable experience.